The Cook's Bible of
INGREDIENTS

The Cook's Bible of
INGREDIENTS

Margaret Brooker

NEW
HOLLAND

First published in 2005 by New Holland Publishers
London • Cape Town • Sydney • Auckland
www.newhollandpublishers.com

Garfield House	80 McKenzie St	14 Aquatic Drive	218 Lake Rd
86 Edgware Rd	Cape Town	Frenchs Forest NSW	Northcote
London W2 2EA	8001	2086	Auckland
United Kingdom	South Africa	Australia	New Zealand

PUBLISHING MANAGERS Claudia Dos Santos & Simon Pooley

COMMISSIONING EDITOR Alfred LeMaitre

EDITOR Gill Gordon

DESIGNER Geraldine Cupido

PICTURE RESEARCHER Karla Kik

PRODUCTION Myrna Collins

PROOFREADER Elizabeth Wilson

CONSULTANTS Sarah Jane Evans, Beverly LeBlanc

ISBN 1 84537 039 2

Reproduction by Resolution Colour (Pty) Ltd, Cape Town
Printed in Singapore by Tien Wah Press (Pte) Ltd

1 3 5 7 9 10 8 6 4 2

Contents

Introduction

Ingredients matter. As the component parts of composite food, ingredients are fundamental to its ultimate quality. Not only should they themselves be of good quality, they should be suitable for their purpose. To cook well, a cook needs to understand the attributes of ingredients he or she is using. The aroma, taste, texture and colour of an ingredient, how it interacts with other ingredients, how it responds to heat, air, liquid or acid, for example, all affect the end result.

With the advent of modern methods of food transportation and conservation, a cook has an ever-increasing, and often bewildering, choice of ingredients; ingredients hitherto only available in their place of origin are now on offer in far flung markets. This affords the home cook much greater scope, and requires more knowledge.

The Cook's Bible is intended to help the cook identify and appreciate the salient characteristics of a multitude of ingredients. A visual reference, with photographs supported by explanatory captions, it will benefit both novice and more experienced, enquiring cooks. Anyone who has occasion to ask 'what food is that?', 'what is its flavour?', or 'how is it used?' will find it enlightening.

In scope this book is international, catering for cooks worldwide, both in the ingredients featured, and the terms of their descriptions. The world of ingredients is vast. Within the numerous food categories and species, there are many variants and sub-species. It would be impossible to include every known ingredient individually in a single book. However, by featuring representative ingredients from a category, this book is as comprehensive as possible.

Such breadth of subjects necessarily imposes limitations of space. Within this constraint, the maximum of information useful to the cook is imparted in a succinct yet accurate manner. As appropriate, the nature of the ingredient, its particular properties, its place of origin, the way it is prepared, and its applications in cookery are described. Common and alternative names are given, and regional variations in nomenclature are clarified. Flavour profiles can be especially difficult to describe. How flavours are perceived is essentially subjective; the descriptions seek to convey sufficient of an impression to enable the cook to judge whether an ingredient is suitable.

The book is arranged in the order of the recommended dietary food pyramid, commencing with grains and cereals and foods made with those ingredients, progressing through vegetables, fruits, pulses and seeds, dairy products and cheeses, meat, poultry and fish to flavourings and sweeteners. Within each chapter the ingredients are logically grouped by type.

RIGHT *Fresh, seasonal ingredients should form an essential part of daily meal planning. They can be supplemented and enhanced by items from a well-stocked pantry.*

Along with understanding an ingredient, the cook should appreciate the factors which influence its quality. Generally its source is of utmost importance. In the case of ingredients where freshness is vital, such as vegetables, fruits and fish, less time is likely to have elapsed between being harvested and reaching the market with local ingredients than those from further afield. Less time in transit also means that they can be picked riper, and so reach their full potential of flavour and sweetness, as well as arrive in better condition.

Foods raised in their natural environments and at their own pace are usually better. Grown in soil, not hydroponically, sun-ripened, not hot-housed, fruits and vegetables achieve greater depth of flavour. Livestock raised free range, without growth promotants, also develops more texture and flavour. It follows, therefore, that produce out of season is either not local or not naturally grown and, conversely that seasonal food is always likely to be better.

Without detailed labelling, it may be difficult for the purchaser to know where and how an ingredient has been produced. Shopping at local and farmer's markets, as well as at reputable food stores with well-informed staff will obviate this problem to a degree.

Supplied with good quality ingredients and informed of their salient attributes, any cook can go into the kitchen and prepare meals with confidence. More than merely inform, it is hoped that the Cook's Bible will encourage and inspire cooks to experiment with the world of ingredients.

LEFT *Markets always offer the freshest seasonal produce available locally, as well as being a source of less-common ingredients that are sometimes hard to find.*

Grains & Cereals

Cereals are plants of the grass family. The many separate dry fruits they produce are grains. Certain cereal grains are edible. Used as a food since the earliest times, cereal grains have been hugely important in human history. Their small bulk and excellent keeping qualities made them a crucial survival food. As the first plants to be cultivated, their domestication marked the transition of humans from hunter-gatherers to agriculturalists and enabled the foundation of civilizations. Cereal grains continue to be essential human fare and today constitute the most important single class of food in the world.

As a plant's embryonic offspring, packaged with food for its development, cereal grains are concentrated sources of nourishment. They contain protein and either carbohydrates or fats. However, all grains are deficient in one or more of the essential amino acids, making them an incomplete protein source for animals.

All grains have the same basic structure. Beneath the protective fibrous outer layers, collectively called 'bran', is the endosperm, which comprises most of the grain's volume and stores most of its carbohydrate and protein. At the base of the endosperm is the oil-rich embryo or 'germ'. Both the bran and the germ contain B-group vitamins and minerals.

Cereals are principally consumed cooked; as grain, they are often eaten in the form of porridge, or as various bread doughs, ground into flour.

Although cereals have many common characteristics, their individual differences have resulted in diverse culinary traditions. Staple cereals differ with geographic zones. Their adaptability to local conditions, yield, and comparative culinary qualities, determined their distribution, as cereals native to one region were introduced elsewhere.

Wheat became the foremost cereal due to the unique quality of its protein. The gluten that forms when wheat flour is mixed with water both resists and stretches under pressure. Because it can expand to accommodate gases produced by yeast, yet contain them, wheat breads can be leavened (caused to rise).

Pseudo-cereals, while not grasses, have a similar nutrient composition to cereals and are treated as such.

Jasmine rice

A slender, long-grained, aromatic white rice, which clings together slightly when cooked. Grown predominantly in Thailand, where it is the preferred variety, it is also known as Thai or Fragrant rice.

Black Thai rice

A long-grained rice with its black bran intact which, cooked, colours the entire grain purple. Also called Black Sticky and Black Glutinous rice, it is typically used for desserts in SE Asia.

White long-grained rice

Long-grained types of rice from which the bran coat has been completely removed. When cooked, the grains generally remain separate and become fluffy-looking. (See also white short-grain rice on p15.)

Brown long-grained rice

Long-grained types of rice which retain their bran layers. Also called whole and unprocessed, brown rice is often heat-treated to slow rancidity of the bran. It requires longer cooking than white rice.

Basmati rice

An aromatic, narrow, very long-grained variety grown in northern India; valued for its fragrant flavour and firm texture. When cooked, the grains remain separate and dry. The rice for biriani and pilaf.

Wild rice

Now cultivated, a black/brown, elongated, hard seed of a marsh grass native to the Great Lakes region of N. America, distantly related to common rice. Expensive, it is appreciated for its chewy, nutty quality.

Mixed brown and wild rice

A mixture of long-grained brown rice and wild rice, both chewy textured and nutty-flavoured, usually combined to extend the more expensive wild rice. Used in pilafs, stuffings and salads.

White short-grained rice
Round, short-grained types of rice, with the bran coat completely removed. The grains cook to a soft consistency and cling together. Also called pudding rice.

Brown short-grained rice
Round, short-grained rices which retain their bran layer. As well as sharing the general characteristics of unpolished rice, the grains become soft and sticky on cooking.

Arborio
A plump, large-grained, starchy Italian rice, graded *superfino*. Able to absorb a lot of liquid without bursting, it is particularly used for risotto.

Vialone nano
A plump, medium-grained, starchy Italian rice, graded *fino*, particularly used for risotto due to its capacity to absorb twice its weight in liquid without bursting.

Carnaroli
Dubbed 'the king of Italian rice', this large-grained starchy rice, graded *superfino*, remains firm while absorbing much liquid, so is prized for risotto.

Sushi
Stubby, short-grained white rice with a high starch content which becomes sticky when cooked. Flavoured with sweetened vinegar, it forms the basis of Japanese sushi.

Red rice
A hard, unmilled rice; actually russet-hued, due to the colour of the bran layer. The French Camargue variety is short-grained, chewy, nutty and slightly sticky when cooked.

White sticky rice
Mostly short-grained rice that becomes sticky when cooked. Also known as glutinous or sweet rice, it is used mainly for desserts.

Rice flour
Powdery, finely ground rice, non-glutinous or glutinous. Entirely starch, with no gluten-forming proteins, it is used as a thickening agent, to make crunchy coatings and in baked goods for crispness.

Poha
Very light flakes with jagged edges and a rough texture, made by flattening parboiled rice grains with rollers, then drying them. An Indian ingredient, also called pawa or pounded rice, the flakes are fried or cooked in milk.

Rice flakes
Parboiled rice which has been flattened under heavy rollers, then dried. The resultant fine flakes are used by the food processing industry.

Ground rice
Coarsely ground, non-glutinous rice. Used for its crisp granular texture in, for example, classic Scottish shortbread and, for its thickening properties, in the Indian blancmange firni. Roasted, it is sprinkled over Thai and Vietnamese dishes.

RICE BRAN
The outer seed-coat of the rice grain, rubbed off after removal of the hull during milling and processing. Rich in oils and vitamins, rice bran quickly becomes rancid unless defatted. Stabilized, it is used in food manufacture for its foaming qualities.

In Japan, rice bran is roasted to extract the flavour, then mixed with water and salt, before being used to pickle vegetables such as daikon, cucumber and carrot.

Corn flakes
A breakfast cereal, made by rolling then toasting cooked grits, the coarsely ground endosperm of corn or maize. Light and crisp when dry, they are principally consumed doused with milk.

Popcorn
A variety of maize, the starchy interior of which cooks and swells when heated, the pressure eventually bursting the kernel and turning it inside-out. Typically the light crisp puffy white kernels are salted and eaten as a snack.

Cornmeal
Ground dried maize (corn) kernels, termed cornmeal in the UK and corn-flour in the USA. It may be fine or coarse in texture, depending on the milling, and yellow, white or blue, depending upon the variety of maize, blue being softer and less starchy.

Cornflour
A fine powder made from the ground endosperm of maize kernels, known as cornflour in the UK and cornstarch in the USA. Almost pure starch, and containing no lump-forming gluten, it is mainly used as a thickening agent. Virtually flavourless.

Polenta
Cornmeal, fine or coarse, yellow or white. A staple of N. Italy, it is traditionally boiled with water to make a thick porridge, and either served warm, or cooled then fried, grilled or baked.

Rye flour

Milled from a hardy cereal grass, rye flour is historically the bread-making staple of northern Europe and Nordic regions and is the defining ingredient in pumpernickel, black bread and crispbread. With a faintly bitter flavour, it is grey in colour, either light or dark according to the amount of bran remaining. Because rye is low in gluten, breads made from only rye flour are dense. A moisture-trapping gum in the grain gives rye doughs a characteristic stickiness and keeps the bread moist.

Rye flakes

Flakes formed by flattening whole rye grains between rollers. Also called rolled rye, the flakes are cooked as a breakfast porridge or toasted and added to commercial breakfast cereals. Due to their unusual configuration, the sugars in rye break down very slowly to simple sugar and thus take a long time to digest, effectively reducing appetite.

Pearl barley
Barley grains with their husks and pellicles (outer layers) removed, then steamed and polished until round and shiny. Pearl barley, the most common form, is used to thicken stews and soups, notably Scotch broth, and has little taste of its own. Pot barley, which has had some of the bran removed, requires long cooking to soften it.

Barley flakes
The flakes produced by flattening whole grains of barley, outer husks removed, between rollers. Used to make milk puddings, porridge and added to breakfast cereals such as muesli, they have a distinct flavour and are slightly chewy. Flakes may be softened by soaking before being used in baked products.

Barley flour
Ground and powdered pearl barley. Because barley contains little gluten, leavened breads made with only barley flour are dense and heavy. Most barley breads are unleavened griddle breads. For leavened breads, barley flour is best mixed with wheat flour. Lacking the water-retaining properties of the gluten network, barley bread goes stale quickly. Barley meal is a wholemeal flour that is coarsely ground from hulled barley.

Whole-wheat flour

Milled from the entire wheat kernel, whole-wheat flour contains all of the grain's bran, germ and endosperm. Also known as wholemeal and, in the USA, graham flour, it is used for baking and general cooking. In unbaked doughs the fibrous bran pierces the gluten network, damaging its structure. Thus breads and cakes made with whole-wheat, rather than refined, flour rise less and bake to a closer texture.

Wheat flakes

The large, thick, firm flakes produced when whole-wheat kernels are steamed, then flattened between rollers. Because the flakes retain the bran and germ, most of the kernel's nutrition remains, although the oils in the germ rapidly become rancid. Also called rolled wheat, the flakes, like rolled oats, are cooked as porridge or added to baked goods.

Wheat germ

The small flakes milled from the embryo, or germ, which is separated from the wheat grain during the milling of white flour. Rich in nutrients, it is added to baked goods and break-fast cereals, or sprinkled over dishes, adding a nutty flavour. Because the germ's high oil content causes it rapidly to become rancid, it should be stored airtight, and chilled.

Unbleached wheat flour

Creamy coloured flour which has not undergone an artificial bleaching process. As it ages, wheat flour naturally bleaches from the oxygen in the air, resulting not only in bread with a whiter crumb but also a greater volume, plus a finer, softer crumb. Bleached flour is treated with oxidizing agents to simulate this process, albeit more quickly.

Wheatmeal

Wheat flour containing 80 to 90 percent of the whole grain, the bulk of the bran being removed in milling but much of the germ remaining. In colour, flavour, baking and keeping qualities, it falls midway between wholewheat and white flours. Wheatmeal is also known as brown flour.

White flour

A fine powder, ground principally from the starchy endosperm of the wheat grain, with almost all the bran and germ removed during milling. For baking, flour is distinguished by degrees of hardness; the harder the flour the more gluten-forming proteins it contains. Thus hard flour, called strong flour in the UK, and bread flour or hard flour in the USA, is better for yeast-raised products, while weaker, soft flour, called plain or all-purpose flour in the UK, and cake flour or soft flour in the USA, being more able to absorb fat, is better for cakes and short pastry.

Wheat bran

Flakes, fine or coarse, of the fibrous outer layer of the wheat grain, separated during milling. Consisting mostly of indigestible cellulose, bran is consumed for the health benefits of roughage. However, its consumption does have a negative effect. The fibre renders bran's high concentrations of minerals and vitamins digestively unavailable and its phytic acid impairs the absorption of calcium. Bran is sprinkled over fruit, or added to breakfast cereals, and baked goods such as breads, biscuits and muffins.

Cracked wheat
Whole-wheat grains broken into coarse, medium or fine fragments during milling. Also called kibbled wheat, it is added, soaked, to bread.

Bulgar wheat
Hulled wheat grains, steamed, dried, then crushed in coarse or fine grades. A Middle Eastern staple, also known as burghul, bulgur, pourgouri and pligouri, it is the basis of tabbouleh and kibbeh.

Atta flour
A fine wholemeal flour made from soft, low gluten wheat. Used to make Indian flatbreads, it is also called chapati flour.

ARAB SPECIALITIES

Two wheat products little known beyond Arab countries, where they are specialties, are Freekah and Moghrabbiyeh.

Freekah, or ferek, is roasted green wheat. Bunches of freshly harvested green wheat stalks are roasted over an open fire and the cooled ears shucked. The grain is either left whole or coarsely cracked: when cracked it is greenish-brown with a distinct smoky taste; whole it is brown and relatively bland. Both forms are cooked like rice or bulgar.

Moghrabbiyeh (maghrebia, Israeli couscous), is flour and water hand-rolled into balls the size of small peas, then dried. Typically they are cooked in broth.

Trahana
A Greek pasta of dough made from flour and milk (sometimes sour), grated into tiny barley-shaped pellets, then dried. Traditionally it is used in soups and porridge.

Couscous

Tiny pellets made from semolina flour, moistened with salted water and hand-rubbed with flour until coated, then dried. To cook, the granules are steamed until swollen and fluffy, with each granule separate. The staple dish of the Maghreb (Northwest Africa), it is traditionally cooked in a couscoussier over a fruity, spicy meat stew with which it is served. Elsewhere, couscous is likely to be pre-cooked and requires only swelling in boiling water.

Semolina flour

Semolina is the coarsely ground endosperm of hard wheat, usually durum wheat. Semolina flour is a finer ground version, sometimes called durum flour. With its high protein content, semolina flour is characteristically tough. Its granularity gives a light, crumbly texture to baked goods. Because it does not become a starchy paste when cooked, it is used to make dried pasta, yet it is also used as a thickener.

Groats

Grain which has been hulled and, usually, coarsely crushed. While 'groats' can denote any such grain, unqualified in the UK it generally refers to oats. In the USA 'grits' is the more common term. High protein and fat content make oats among the most nutritious of cereals. However, unless steam-treated, the fat, combined with an enzyme in the bran, rapidly causes rancidity. Groats can be prepared as porridge or like rice.

Rolled oats

Oats which have been hulled, steam-softened, then rolled flat. The heating destroys the enzymes in the bran which would otherwise cause the fat in the germ to go rancid. Rolled oats therefore keep well. The various sizes of flakes depend upon whether the whole groat or pinhead oatmeal was rolled. As well as relatively fast-cooking porridge, rolled oats are used in muesli and biscuits.

Oat bran

Fine pale-brown flakes of the thin, fibre-rich layer of cells located under the rough outer hull of the groat, more accurately named oat fibre. Because the adherent layer is impossible to remove cleanly, small creamy fragments of the nutritious centre of the grain speckle the fibre. Containing significant water-soluble dietary fibre, oat bran is consumed for its cholesterol-reducing properties and added to baked goods.

Oat flour

A fine powder ground from husked oats, distinct from super-fine oatmeal which still has a granule. It is used for general baking but, with no gluten-forming proteins of its own, for risen baked goods it must be combined with another flour that contains gluten-forming proteins. Because oat flour includes the germ and the bran, which together rapidly go rancid, it does not keep well and should be freshly ground.

Oatmeal

Granules of milled oat grains processed to varying grades of fineness. For the coarsest, pinhead meal, the groat is cut into several pieces. When ground, pinhead progressively becomes rough, medium-rough, medium, fine and super-fine oatmeal. Unless heat-treated, oatmeal does not keep well, rapidly going rancid. An historical staple of Scotland, oatmeal is primarily used in porridge and oatcakes, and is a key ingredient in Atholl brose and haggis.

Buckwheat

Though botanically not a true cereal, buckwheat is treated as such. Once husked, the whole seeds, which are triangular in cross section with pointed ends, may be cooked in the same way as rice, most famously in kasha, the porridge-like dish of Russia. Ground into a black-flecked greyish flour, it is made into pancakes, notably Russian blini and Breton galettes, noodles, especially the Japanese speciality soba, and cakes. It has a strong, distinctive taste.

Quinoa

Pronounced 'keen wa', these are tiny discs of grain girded by a small band of bran. A staple of the Andes, this pseudo-cereal has a high concentration of amino acids so, unlike other grains, it is a complete protein. When cooked it expands to four times its original volume and becomes translucent, the bran visible as a curly tail. Cooked quinoa has a delicate flavour and a texture akin to caviar, and can be served like rice, couscous or millet. The uncooked seeds can be ground into flour.

Sago

The virtually pure starch extracted from the sago palm, which is made into a paste and dried to become sago flour or pressed through a sieve, then dried, to become pellets known as pearl sago. Cooked, sago turns from white to transparent, and is bland, its texture resiliently squishy. The basis of British nursery puddings, sago is now little used in Western cooking. In Asia, sago is used in both forms, notably with coconut milk and palm sugar in the dessert gula melaka.

Tapioca

The starch extracted from the roots of cassava or manioc plants, which are refined to a paste, dried, then heated to form flakes or pellets, called pearls, or ground into flour. Used in puddings and to thicken soups and stews, tapioca becomes translucent when cooked, gelatinously chewy in texture and has a subtle taste. In some Asian countries, it is much used in sweets and drinks. In the UK, it is historically known as the ingredient in a milk pudding.

Linseed

The tiny seed of the flax plant, also known as flax seed. Primarily used to produce oil, it is sometimes used as a food grain, sprinkled over dishes and mixed into baked goods, sprouted, or ground into flour, which becomes mucilaginous (glutinous) when wet. Rich in nutrients, especially omega-3 fatty acids, linseed is consumed more for its health benefits than its mildly nutty taste. Its high oil content means it goes rancid quickly.

Millet

The general name applied to many similar but distinct cereals, most of which have alternative names. All are very small grains, with a high protein content, but otherwise vary in their quality and flavour. They are consumed whole, or ground into a coarse flour, typically as porridge or flatbreads. Able to grow in poor conditions, millet is a staple in hot, dry regions but not much eaten in western countries.

Soya flour

A fine creamy-yellow powder ground from grits of hulled soya beans from which the oil and soluble carbohydrates have been removed. Although it contains no gluten-forming proteins, it is rich in other forms of protein and fat and low in carbohydrates, and is usually mixed with other flours to improve the protein, volume and keeping-quality of baked goods. Food manufacturers exploit its binding qualities. In Japan, where it is called *kinako*, it is used for confectionery.

Potato flour

A very fine, brilliant white powder made by grinding either steamed, dried potatoes or the starch extracted from pulverized potatoes by a washing process. Also called potato starch, farina and, in France, *fécule*, it is used as a thickener, producing clear, light sauces. Being more effective than cereal starches, less is required. It is used in baked goods for its gluten-free status and for the moist crumb it gives.

Urad

A creamy-white powder ground from hulled urad or urd black lentils, also known as black gram. It is the basis of the traditional idlis (dumplings) and dosas (pancakes) of South India and is also used to make poppadoms.

Spelt

An ancient, non-hybridized cereal grain related to common wheat, also known by the German name of *dinkel*. It contains more protein, and thus forms more gluten, than common wheat, yet seems to be better tolerated by those with gluten allergies. Ground into flour, spelt can be substituted for common wheat flour and behaves like whole-wheat flour, imparting a distinct nutty, wheaty flavour.

Arrowroot

A fine white powder extracted from the rhizomes of the tropical maranta plant. Containing 80 per cent starch, it is used as a thickener for sauces and glazes. Because it becomes clear when cooked and has no taste, it is considered superior to cornflour. To avoid lumps it should be slaked in cold liquid before cooking. It breaks down if overcooked, causing sauces to separate. Easily digestible, it is a traditional food for invalids

Matzo meal

Crumbled matzos, the thin unleavened Jewish Passover bread made according to strict regulations to avoid any fermentation, from wheat flour and water. Available in fine and medium grinds, it is used like breadcrumbs, as a thickener for soups, to bind gefilte fish, for breading foods to be fried, as an ingredient in dumplings (matzo balls or knaidlach) and, soaked and squeezed dry, in cakes and pancakes.

Noodles & Pasta

Noodles, pasta and flatbreads are essentially doughs made from starch and water, thinly shaped and quickly cooked. The many permutations of these basic features give rise to a huge diversity in all three foods.

'Noodles' is a generic term encompassing both the various oriental pastas and certain occidental pastas. The commonality of noodles and pastas is often attributed to them having a single origin. Although the origins are unknown, the theory that Marco Polo introduced pasta to Italy from China has been discredited; pasta existed in Europe before the 14th century. Noodles are such a simple concept that their discovery by more than one culture is likely.

Asian noodles are categorized by their major ingredient. The diversity of their various starch bases results in very different flavours and textures. In shape they vary between wide and narrow, flat and round, thin and fat, but are always long.

Pasta, conversely, is always made from wheat flour or semolina; hard wheat flour, often mixed with eggs, is used for fresh pasta, and the even harder durum wheat semolina preferred for dried, commercial pasta. There are over 300 pasta shapes, which may be generally classified as long, short (which includes soup shapes or 'pastine'), and filled. Most shapes are named, in Italian, after the object they resemble, their size often further described by diminutives and superlatives. Confusingly, nomenclature is not standard. Particular pastas suit certain styles of sauce. Basically, the sauce should adhere to the pasta, yet not overwhelm it. Both the delicacy of the pasta, relative to the sauce, and its shape must be considered; ribbed ('rigate') and hollow shapes trap sauce best.

Flatbreads were the earliest form of bread. Originally primitive pastes crudely baked on a hot surface, they evolved into a multiplicity of breads. Variously made from different grains, tubers and legumes, leavened and unleavened, and baked in ovens and skillets, grilled and fried, they range from parchment thin to relatively thick, brittle to pliable. Their defining characteristic is that they are flat.

Soba (buckwheat) noodles

Slender noodles, square in cross section, made with buckwheat flour or, more usually, buckwheat and wheat flour, water and salt. Nutty flavoured, soba vary in shades of mushroom brown, the darkest (*yabu soba*) being made from the whole grain and the palest and most prized (*gozen soba*) from the kernel. A speciality of northern Japan and Tokyo, soba are typically served cold with a dipping sauce, or hot in soup. Pale green *chasoba* are flavoured with green tea.

Egg noodles

Golden noodles made from a paste of wheat flour, water and egg, extruded into round and flat ribbon shapes of varying widths. The classic fine strands (pictured) may be fresh or dried, while the fatter versions, such as the thick, round Hokkien noodles, are sold fresh and often oiled. Already steamed, egg noodles require little cooking. The all-purpose Chinese noodles, they are also used throughout Asia in soups, and stir fries, enjoyed for their rich flavour and soft texture.

Somen

Very fine, creamy-white, straight Japanese noodles made from wheat flour, salt, water and oil, generally sold dried, in even-length bundles. Formed by pulling the dough, somen differ from other Japanese noodles, which are rolled then cut. Somen are a summer food, traditionally served chilled.

Wheat noodles

Thin, pale strands of various widths made, at their most basic, from a dough of wheat flour and water. Often flavoured with ingredients such as shrimp, crab or spinach, wheat noodles are sold fresh or, more commonly, dried. They are versatile noodles, inherently resilient, and readily absorb flavours. In northern China, where they originated, they are typically served in soups or stir-fried.

Udon

Plump, white Japanese noodles made from a dough of wheat flour and water, and sometimes vinegar to make them whiter. Udon are formed in various dimensions: the fresh ones are usually fat and square-cut, while the dried versions may be flat, square or round in cross section. Neutral in flavour, their character is in their texture – soft, chewy and slippery. Udon are popular in the south of Japan, where traditionally they are served in soups.

PREPARING NOODLES

Noodles are generally boiled, or reconstituted in boiling water, until they are softened but still firm, before further preparation.

Rice vermicelli

Fine, dried, brittle noodles made from an extruded paste of rice flour and water. Translucent when dry, when cooked they become opaque. Vermicelli are versatile, used throughout Asia in soups, stir fries and spring rolls to add texture and contrast; either soft or deep-fried until crisp, their neutral taste is a vehicle for strong flavours. The Chinese call rice vermicelli 'rice sticks', but see below.

Rice stick noodles

Dried, brittle, flat ribbon noodles ranging in width from narrow to broad. Made from a paste of rice flour and water, like rice vermicelli, they are translucent when dry, becoming opaque when cooked. Though similarly bland in taste, being thicker they are more robust and elastic. Rice sticks are commonly used in Vietnam and Thailand, notably in the famous *pad Thai*.

Bean thread noodles

Fine, wiry, shimmering, translucent noodles extruded from a paste of mung bean starch and water. Extremely tough when dry, they need soaking before cooking (unless deep-frying) when they become glassy and transparent, with a gelatinous, slithery texture. They absorb a lot of cooking liquid so, being relatively tasteless, take on its flavours. Used throughout Asia in spring rolls, soups, braised dishes and desserts, their many names include cellophane, glass, jelly, silver and shining noodles.

Bean curd noodles

Brittle, shiny, plastic-looking tubes cut from the thin, golden, crinkly sheets of dried bean curd, made by drying either thin layers of compressed soya bean curds or the skin which forms on top of heated soya milk. Unless being added to broth, they should be reconstituted in water before use. To eat they are rubbery and bland, with an almost-smoky aroma. Also called soya noodles.

Rice papers

Thin, brittle sheets, round, square or wedge-shaped, made from a rice and water paste and textured with the basket-weave imprint of their bamboo drying mats. They become flexible when moistened with water. They are used to wrap the spring rolls of Vietnam (where they are called *bahn trang*) and Thailand.

Wonton wrappers

Paper-thin squares (typically 8cm/3in) of smooth pastry made from plain flour, salt, egg and cold water. Sold stacked, dusted with flour to prevent them sticking together, they are used to make wontons (Chinese dumplings). They are also called wonton skins.

Mandarin pancakes

Thin, round Chinese pancakes made from plain flour and boiling water and cooked on a dry griddle. Steamed, they are the traditional accompaniment to Peking duck, and are also used to wrap other savoury mixtures.

Chinese dumpling wrappers

Thicker sheets of pastry made from plain wheat flour and water. Also known
as 'gow gee wrappers', they are used to wrap Chinese dumplings (*gyoza*)
and for other savoury fillings.

Sushi wrapper

Paper-thin, glossy, rectangular sheets of dried seaweed, of the genus *Pophyra*,
ranging in colour from purplish-black to green. Toasted, as it should be before
use, it becomes dark green, crisp and more flavoursome, and is called
yaki-nori. It is also sold ready-toasted. Most commonly used to wrap the
Japanese vinegared rice speciality, sushi, when it is called *sushi-nori*, it is
also crumbled over other foods to add flavour. (See also p198.)

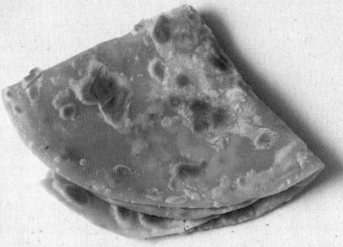

Chapati/roti

A round, unleavened everyday bread of the Indian subcontinent, made from atta flour, salt and water, and cooked without fat on a griddle, until puffed. Roti is also a general term for griddle-cooked flat unleavened bread and takes many forms.

Poppadom/papadam/papadum

Wafer-thin Indian flatbread discs made of lentil or cereal flours, sometimes spiced. Sun-dried until brittle, then roasted or fried until crisp and puffed, they is served as an accompaniment.

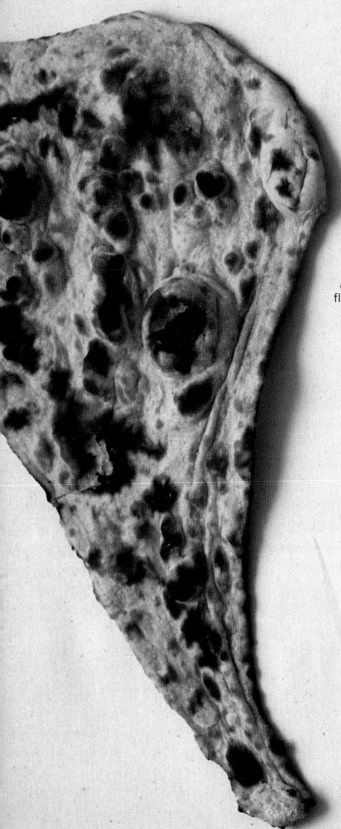

Naan/nan

A flattened, natural yeast-leavened wheat bread of India and Central Asia. Traditionally cooked slapped against the clay walls of a tandoor oven, naan is teardrop-shaped, puffy and blackened, with a crisp crust, soft centre and smoky flavour.

Taco shell

A corn tortilla folded in half and deep-fried to a crisp U-shape. Adapted by Tex-Mex cuisine, taco shells are typically filled with minced (ground) meat, shredded lettuce, grated cheese and salsa, and eaten as a snack.

Ciabatta

A free-form stubby bread, originally from Como (Italy), named for the slipper-shape it resembles. The very wet dough, which contains both milk and olive oil, results in a light, porous chewy crumb with large holes and a thin crust.

Focaccia

A rustic flattened, leavened regional Italian bread made with yeast, flour and water, seasoned with olive oil and herbs, its dimpled surface drizzled with oil and sprinkled with toppings.

Matzah/matzo

Thin, crisp unleavened bread, traditionally eaten at the Jewish Passover to commemorate the hasty flight from Egypt. As it must not ferment, no more than 18 minutes may elapse from mixing the flour and water until it is baked.

Tortilla

Round, thin, soft, pliable, brown-speckled, creamy-white unleavened bread. A Mexican staple, tortillas are made from a dough of masa (flour ground from dried corn) or wheat flour, shaped and pressed, then cooked on a hot ungreased griddle, and eaten plain, or wrapped around various fillings, as in burritos and enchiladas.

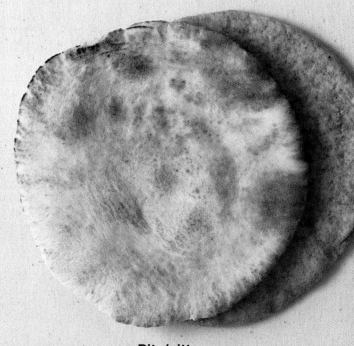

Pita/pitta

A round or oval, flat, slightly leavened Middle Eastern wheat bread with an internal pocket that forms during baking. Soft-crusted, dense and chewy, it is split open and stuffed, used as a scoop, or toasted for fattoush, a traditional bread salad.

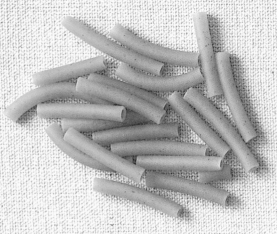

Macaroni

The anglicized version of the Italian *maccheroni*, a hollow, tubular, short, sturdy dried pasta of various sizes. It may be straight or 'elbow' (curved).

Farfalle

A sturdy pasta named for the butterflies its shape resembles, sometimes also called bow ties.

Fusilli

A sturdy pasta twisted into a spiral or twist, either long or short, and in the case of fusilli bucati, hollow.

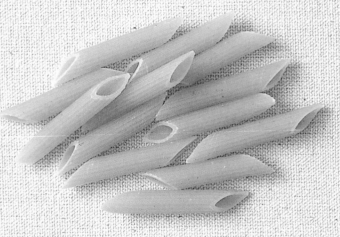

Penne

Short lengths of hollow, tubular sturdy pasta cut diagonally at both ends like the quill pens for which it is named.

Conchiglie

A sturdy pasta shaped like the conch-shell for which it is named. Its surface may be ribbed or smooth.

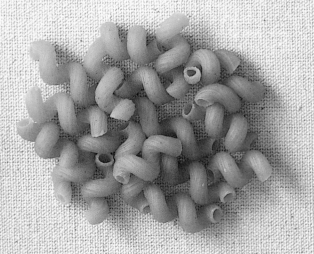

Cavatappi

Short lengths of hollow, tubular, sturdy pasta, spiralled like corkscrews, for which they are named.

Gnocchi

Hollow, shell-like shapes, ridged on their convex surface, with a closer resemblance to conchiglie than gnocchi (see p44).

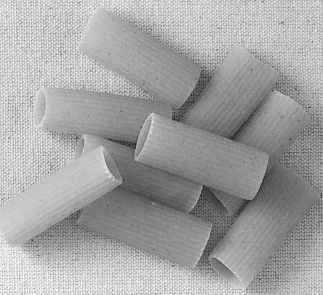

Rigatoni

Large hollow sturdy tubes of pasta with a grooved exterior surface.

Rotelli/ruote

Small wheels of dried pasta, with hubs, spokes and smooth or grooved rims. Rotelli also denotes a spiral pasta.

Animaletti

Dried pasta extruded in the form of various animal shapes; appealing to children.

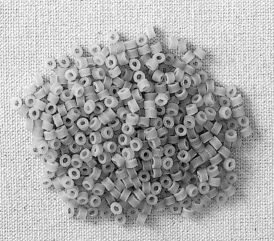

Tubettini

Very short lengths of small, hollow, dried pasta, literally called 'tiny tubes', typically used in light soups.

Orzo

Small pasta, shaped like grains of rice, although named after barley. It is especially used in soup.

Spaghetti

Long, thin, round, solid rods, literally called 'thin strings'. The most universally popular form of pasta, and among the most versatile, spaghetti is made in several thicknesses, often graded by number.

Linguine

Long, thin, solid rods of dried pasta, oval in section, like flattened spaghetti, literally called 'little tongues'; also known as bavetti.

Fettuccine

Long, flat, strips or ribbons of pasta, fresh or dried, about 9mm (⅜in) wide. Fettuccine is the Roman version of tagliatelle but traditionally is narrower and slightly thicker. (*Fettuccia* means small ribbons.)

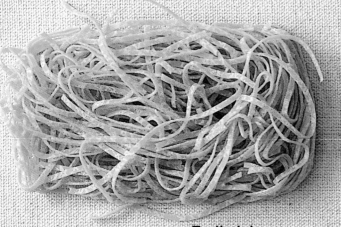

Tagliarini

Long thin flat ribbons of fresh pasta, usually less than 3mm (⅛in) wide; the narrowest member of the tagliatelle family.

Vermicelli

Long, fine, round, solid rods of dried pasta. Called vermicelli, literally 'little worms'; in southern Italy, this thinner version of spaghetti is also called spaghettini.

Tagliolini

Long, flat, paper-thin, very narrow ribbons of fresh or dried (as here) pasta, usually about 6mm (¼in) wide. Part of the tagliatelle family of cut pasta, tagliolini is a wider version of tagliarini.

Bavettini

Long, thin, solid rods of dried pasta, oval in section, a finer version of linguine/bavetti (see above).

Capelli d'angelo
Long, extremely fine strands of pasta, literally called 'angel's hair'. Normally sold as a nest or bundle, capelli d'angelo is used in soup or with a very light sauce.

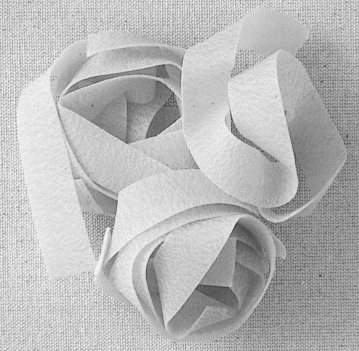

Lasagne
Very wide, flat, rectangular, thin sheets of fresh or dried pasta, sometimes with one or both edges ruffled (*riccie*). Lasagne is mainly used in baked dishes.

Pappardelle
Broad, flat ribbons of pasta, fresh or dried, often with a fluted edge. Of Tuscan origin, they traditionally accompany hare stew and go well with hearty meat-based sauces.

Bucatini
Long, thin, tubular rods of pasta, like thick hollow or pierced spaghetti.

Tagliatelle
Long, flat, thin ribbons of fresh or dried pasta, a little wider than fettuccine. Often hand-made, it is traditionally cut from a rich flour and egg dough.

Gnocchi

Small Italian dumplings, most commonly made of pureed potato mixed with flour and sometimes eggs, and formed by ridging thimble-sized pieces of dough against the tines of a fork or grater. Gnocchi are cooked in boiling water, then dressed, like pasta, with a savoury sauce, or with melted butter and parmesan.

Ravioli

Pillow-like rectangles or squares of thinly rolled fresh egg pasta dough, cut with crenellated edges, and stuffed with a variety of fillings, including meat, vegetables or cheese. They are served in broth, or boiled and then dressed with a sauce, or simply topped with butter and cheese.

Tortellini/tortelloni

Squares or discs of fresh egg pasta, stuffed, then curved into rings, and the edges pinched together so each resembles a navel or hat in shape. Fillings often include ricotta and spinach. Tortelloni are larger versions of tortellini.

Cappelletti

Shaped like little hats, varying in form and filling according to their origin; many stuffings include meat and parmesan. Traditionally they are served in broth or dressed with butter and parmesan. Cappellacci, with a pumkin-based filling, are a large version of cappelletti.

Vegetables & Fungi

'Vegetable' is a culinary term which has no botanical meaning. Although the concept is generally understood, the popular definition of 'vegetable' is imprecise and incomplete. At best a vegetable can be defined as 'a plant, usually herbaceous, of which any part is eaten in savoury dishes'. The edible parts may be leaves, roots, tubers, bulbs, stems, pods, flowers or seeds. Some fruits are also treated as vegetables.

Most vegetables are cultivated, having been developed from wild predecessors. There are a vast number of species, within which are numerous cultivars, each with different properties and differing nutritional profiles, but most are rich in essential nutrients and fibre, while low in fat. Accordingly, vegetables are generally considered a vital part of a well-balanced diet.

With some notable exceptions, vegetables are best eaten freshly picked. Because they continue to live when harvested from the plant, vegetables use their own stored sugar to carry on, and thus their sweetness, flavour and, sometimes, their texture, deteriorates. As they age, water loss causes them to wilt and microbes may spoil them. Locally grown produce is more likely to be freshly picked, while produce in season is likely to be local.

'Fungi' in the vegetable sense denotes mushrooms and truffles. The part eaten is the fruiting body. Primitive organisms, fungi are in a class of their own; as they do not contain chlorophyll they do not photosynthesize sugars so are saprophytic, living symbiotically on the decaying remains of other organisms. They differ from higher plants in composition, their cell walls being made not from cellulose but less-digestible chitin.

Not nutritionally significant, fungi are eaten for their rich, almost meaty, flavour and texture and, in some cases, their unique aroma. They intensify flavours, like a natural version of monosodium glutamate, due to their high content of glutamic acid. Some fungi are cultivated, but most must be gathered wild. This, and their superior flavour, makes wild fungi highly prized. As some are toxic, wild fungi should be positively identified before consumption.

Cos/romaine lettuce

A head lettuce whose elongated green leaves are crisp and coarse, with a succulent mid-rib and a slightly bitter taste. They are classically used in Caesar salad.

Iceberg/crisphead lettuce

A round lettuce with a head of tightly compacted crisp thin leaves. Crunchy but with little taste, they are eaten raw in salads and sandwiches; the cupped leaves are used to contain fillings.

Butterhead lettuce

A category of lettuce with round, loosely formed heads of soft floppy leaves. They have a delicate flavour and a tender, easily bruised texture, suited to light dressings in salads.

Baby gem lettuce

A small lettuce with a compact head of elongated leaves. Crisp, succulent and sweet with excellent flavour, it is served quartered or as leaves, dressed.

Lollo biondo and lollo rosso

Loose-leafed lettuce with soft, frilly-edged green leaves (lollo biondo, left), or progressively coloured red toward the edges (lollo rosso, right). They look attractive but their flavour is dull so they are better mixed with other leaves.

Rocket/arugula

The tooth-edged green leaves of a cress plant. With a pungent peppery bite when raw, they are used as a salad leaf. Young leaves are tender; larger leaves are coarse and more assertive.

Mixed leaves

An assortment of salad leaves, of varied colour, texture and flavour. Depending upon the season it may include green and red oak-leaf, rocket, frisée, radicchio, lamb's lettuce (corn salad, *mâche*), lollo biondo and rosso, and beet leaves. Mixed leaves are sometimes called mesclun.

Baby spinach

The young leaves of *spinacea oleracea*, so tender they may be eaten raw in salads. Cooked, spinach is served as a vegetable and is a versatile ingredient, teaming well with dairy products, its lightly acidic taste complementing delicate dishes. It requires thorough washing before use and wilts when heated, reducing greatly in volume.

Chicory/endive

A forced spindle-shaped 'chicon' with tightly furled leaves blanched white with yellow tips. It is called chicory in the UK, endive or Belgian endive in the USA and France, and witloof in Australasia. Mildly bitter in taste, it is crisp and juicy when eaten raw, softening when cooked.

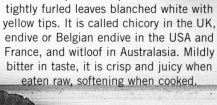

Watercress

A member of the crucifer family, grown in cool shallow waters, watercress has a crisp peppery bite. It is usually eaten raw, in salads, sandwiches and as a garnish, particularly for game. When cooked, in soups or like spinach, it loses its pungency.

Chard

With large, crinkly green leaves and fleshy stems that are commonly creamy white but also red or golden, chard is often cooked as two vegetables. The leaves are like spinach in flavour, but more robust in texture. Its many types include Swiss and ruby chard, silver and seakale beet.

Asparagus

The fleshy young shoots of a cultivated lily plant. A prized spring delicacy, green or purple asparagus is cut above ground and white aparagus grown under the earth. White asparagus is smoother but tougher-skinned, so needs peeling. Their girth increases as the plant matures; thin green shoots are called 'sprue'. Steamed, grilled or roasted, asparagus is served warm or cold, with oil or butter-based sauces.

Celery

Crisp, thick, succulent, leafy cultivated stems, ranging in shades of green, the darker shades being more strongly flavoured. As a vegetable, celery is eaten raw or cooked, often braised or stir-fried. In stocks or sautéed, finely chopped with onion and carrot, it contributes the basic flavouring to many European dishes.

Globe artichoke

The edible flower bud of a thistle. A spring delicacy, when young the whole bud is eaten raw, or cooked. When mature only the base of the petal-like bracts and the bottom, or heart, are eaten (the fibrous central choke is discarded). Artichokes are boiled and served warm or cold with sauces, or stuffed.

Swede
The swollen stem-base, commonly yellow-fleshed, of a cabbage/turnip hybrid, called rutabaga in the USA and neep in Scotland. The buttery purée, 'bashed neeps', traditionally accompanies haggis.

Beetroot
A root, predominantly red and globular, also called garden beet. Eaten raw, or cooked and served hot or cold, its inherent earthy sweetness is often off-set with sour flavours. The leaves can be prepared like spinach.

Radish
A swollen cruciferous root, varying in shape, colour and piquancy. Usually radishes are eaten raw for their pepperiness, in salads or dipped in butter and salt.

Carrot
A root vegetable. Inherently sweet, carrots are eaten raw, cooked as a vegetable, and used as an ingredient in both sweet and savoury dishes.

Celeriac
The bulbous stem-base of a variety of celery, also called turnip-rooted celery and celery-root. Beneath a fibrous skin, it has firm cream flesh tasting mildly of celery. It is eaten raw or cooked, often as a purée, or julienned *en rémoulade*.

Yam
Botanically, an underground stem tuber of the many-specied genus *Dioscorea*. Yams must be cooked to be safe to eat, and are starchy and slightly sweet, with little flavour.

Daikon/Oriental radish

A giant, white-fleshed, mild, oriental radish, called daikon in Japanese and mooli in Hindi. Extensively used in Japan, daikon is eaten raw or cooked (stir-fried, braised, pickled or stewed), and used as a garnish.

Sweet potato

A tropical tuberous root, varying in shape, skin and flesh colours. Starchy and sweet, sometimes mealy, it is eaten boiled, baked, fried, mashed, candied, and used in desserts.

Potatoes

An edible tuber of the nightshade family. The hundreds of potato cultivars vary in shape, size, skin and flesh colours. For cooks the most important distinction is whether potatoes are waxy or floury. Waxy potatoes, high in moisture and low in starch, hold their shape and remain firm when boiled. Conversely, floury potatoes, low in moisture and high in starch, disintegrate when boiled, but bake, mash and roast well. 'Early' (new) potatoes are waxy. 'Main crop' (mature) may be waxy or floury, and may change as a season progresses.

Turnip

A swollen cruciferous stem-base, commonly white fleshed. Best eaten young. Delicately peppery, naturally sweet turnips are braised and glazed by the French, and pickled by Japanese and Arab cooks.

Buttercup squash

A round and ribbed winter squash, with dark green speckled and striped skin. Its fine-textured orange flesh is firm and slightly sweet in flavour. It can be used in the same manner as most winter squash

Pattypan squash

Small summer squash with a scalloped rim, either pale to dark green, white, or deep yellow. Steamed whole, their appealing shape and sweet delicate flesh is preserved. They are also called scallopini, custard marrow and patti pans.

Baby gem squash

Gem squash, picked very young, its skin still soft. Steamed whole, the entire squash, skin, seeds and silken flesh, may be eaten.

Gem squash

A small, round summer squash, with a skin of intermediate hardness. When cooked, the flesh is moist and delicately flavoured. It is ideal for stuffing when the seeds are scooped out.

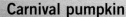

Butternut squash

A winter squash, shaped like an elongated pear, with beige to golden brown skin and dense, bright orange flesh. Dry, sweet and earthy, it is cooked as other winter squash, and is particularly good baked or roasted.

Carnival pumpkin

One of hundreds of varieties of winter squash, ranging in skin colours, size and shape, typically with sweet, orange flesh. While they vary in taste and texture most can be used interchangeably in recipes. Comprising about 90 per cent water winter squash easily become waterlogged, so they are best baked. With their seeds removed they can be stuffed, roasted, puréed for soups, used as a filling in sweet or savoury pies and pasta, and candied.

Pickling cucumber/gherkin

A variety of short, slim cucumbers with dark green, spiny or bumpy skin. They are grown especially for pickling. The immature fruit of long varieties are also pickled.

Ridged cucumber

A short, standard variety of cucumber grown outdoors. Often the relatively tough smooth, dark green skin is peeled and the developed seeds in the crisp, juicy flesh removed. It is also called Green Ridge Cucumber.

Lebanese cucumber

A short cucumber, with dark green, tender skin, and very sweet, extremely juicy, pale green flesh studded with tiny seeds.

English cucumber

A long, slender, cylindrical cucumber with thin, dark green skin and pale, mild, crisp, very juicy, effectively seedless flesh. Also called telegraph, continental, hothouse and 'burpless' cucumber.

Marrow

A large, mature courgette/zucchini, also known as a vegetable marrow. With size, it becomes coarser in texture and more watery, its original delicate flavour diluted to blandness. It is best when halved, deseeded, stuffed and baked.

Baby marrows

A summer squash, also known by their French name courgettes and Italian name zucchini. Cylindrical, sometimes curved, their flecked skins are dark or pale green, or bright yellow, their flesh moist and cream-coloured with tiny seeds. Delicate in flavour, they are eaten unpeeled, raw or cooked; frying, grilling or baking being preferred as they can become waterlogged if boiled.

Red onion
A variety of onion bulb, also called Italian onion, with burgundy coloured skin and decorative red-tinged white flesh. Mild and sweet in flavour, they are often eaten raw, in salads and salsas.

Spring onions
Immature onions with hollow green tops, harvested before the bulb has swollen, also known as green onions and scallions. Mild in flavour and entirely edible, they are eaten both raw and cooked, by quick methods.

Onions
Bulbs consisting of layers of white flesh (tear-inducing when cut), covered in a dry, often golden brown, papery skin. With a pungent bite when raw, transforming to a melting sweetness when gently cooked, onions are mostly used to deepen and sweeten flavours.

Shallots
Clusters of small, elongated bulbs, each covered in papery skin coloured brown to grey to pink. Finely textured with a flavour between onion and garlic, but milder and not astringent, shallots are the epicures' onion.

Leek

An elongated, cylindrical bulb of encircling leaves, white at the base graduating to dark green where the leaves open at the top. Generally only the white and palest green part is used, well washed of harboured soil. Non-astringent, with a mild, sweet onion flavour leeks are eaten cooked, as a dressed vegetable and in soups, stews and tarts.

Garlic

A bulb or 'head' composed of many cloves, each encased in white, mauve or pink papery skin. An important flavouring, especially in Asian and Mediterranean cuisines, raw garlic is fiery, pungent and crunchy; gently cooked, it mellows, becoming mild, sweet and creamy.

Chives

The smallest bulb of the onion family, cultivated as a herb for its thin, tubular, green leaves with their discreet onion tang. Because heat destroys their flavour and colour, chives are best snipped fresh over food just before serving.

Baby leek

A young slender leek, the sweetest. Tender enough to eat whole, cooked baby leeks are often served as an appetiser dressed with vinaigrette, or a cream or tomato-based sauce.

Mung bean sprouts
Newly sprouted mung bean seeds, with a small white root. Mild and crunchy, they are eaten raw or lightly cooked.

Raw peanuts (groundnuts)
Leguminous seeds covered in a papery skin. Comprising up to 55% oil and 30% protein, they are eaten in many forms (see also p91).

Alfalfa sprouts
Wispy shoots of germinated alfalfa or lucerne seeds. Crisp, with a mild pea flavour, they are used raw as a salad vegetable.

Lentil sprouts
Shoots of germinated lentil seeds. With a nutty flavour and a crunchy texture they are eaten raw or lightly cooked.

Corn
The sweet varieties of maize, grown to eat fresh, also called sweetcorn. Husks and 'silk' cover plump white and/or yellow kernels, ranged along a central cob. Consumed on the cob, the kernels also feature in fritters, soups and succotash. Baby corn, harvested before pollination, is entirely edible and is mainly stir-fried.

Peas

Leguminous, round green seeds, podded and eaten fresh. When young, they are tender and sweet. They are also called green, garden and English peas.

Sugar snap peas

Young pea pods plump with developed but tiny peas, so tender the whole pod is eaten. Also called snap, snow and sugar peas, they are cooked briefly to remain crisp.

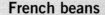

French beans

Long, slender, round, green pods, nowadays usually stringless, encasing small round edible seeds. Eaten fresh as one vegetable, it has many names, including green, snap, haricots and, unjustly, string beans.

Mangetout/snow peas

Almost flat pea pods with tiny bumps of immature peas. The whole pod is eaten, briefly cooked, often stir-fried.

RAW OR COOKED?

Immediately corn and peas are picked, their sugars begin converting to starch, so they are best eaten just-picked.

Raw bean and pea sprouts contain a substance which inhibits the protein-digesting enzyme trypsin, so if eaten in any quantity they should be lightly cooked.

Soya bean sprouts

The long yellowish shoots of germinated soya bean seeds. Relatively strongly flavoured, fibrous and sturdy, they are best when stir-fried.

REDUCE SMELLS

As vegetables of the cabbage family cook, odiferous compounds such as ammonia and hydrogen sulphide are produced. The longer the cooking times, the more compounds are produced, so generally brief cooking is advised for these vegetables.

Cauliflower

A sprouting brassica with one head of tiny white, crisp, tightly-packed flowerbuds, called curds, on clusters of stalks, cupped by crisp green leaves. The florets are eaten raw, or lightly cooked and dressed in a sauce.

Broccoli

A sprouting brassica, most commonly with compact clusters of tightly-packed, dark blue-green flowerbuds, each grouped on its own thick stalk. Also called calabrese and, formerly, 'Italian asparagus', it is usually eaten lightly cooked, and suits creamy sauces.

Pak choi

An oriental brassica, typically a loose cluster of oval green leaves with fleshy white stalks often spoon-shaped at the base, also called bok choy and Chinese white cabbage. Mild but cabbagey in flavour, it is stir-fried, braised and added to soups.

Red cabbage

A brassica with a round, compact head of smooth, purple-red leaves with white veins. To preserve its red colouring when cooked, acidic ingredients are necessary. Traditionally it is braised with wine or vinegar, fruit and spices.

Baby cabbage

A young specimen of the common round tight-headed green cabbage. With the same crisp, pungent character, it can be prepared as a fully grown cabbage, raw, and cooked while its small size suits serving whole.

Tatsoi/tasai

The Japanese name for flat-headed or rosette pak choi. The rounded leaves, stronger flavoured and considered superior to standard pak choi, are stir-fried, braised and added to soups. Young leaves are eaten raw in salads.

Brussels sprouts

Small, compact green brassica buds, resembling miniature cabbages, borne along a single stem, at their best in winter. Typically they are served as a side vegetable, boiled whole, often buttered and teamed with chestnuts.

Savoy cabbage

A round, loose-headed brassica with crisp, crinkly green leaves, progressively paler near the centre. Milder in flavour than smooth-leaved cabbages, it is generally considered the best variety for cooking, variously sautéd, stuffed, steamed, stir-fried and wilted.

Rosa tomato

Baby plum-shaped tomatoes with firm skin and dense flesh. Their intense tomato flavour enhances mixed salads.

Sun-dried tomato

Halved tomatoes, usually plum, salted and dried in the sun. Leathery and intensely flavoured, they need rehydration, in oil or water, before use.

Roma tomato

Elongated, egg-shaped tomatoes, also called plum, Italian and paste tomatoes. With dense, meaty flesh, and relatively little pulp, they are the best for cooking, holding their shape and readily reducing for sauces.

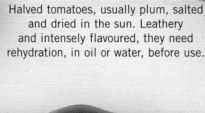

Round/salad tomato

General-purpose tomatoes, typically red, and medium-sized, with large cavities full of juicy seed pulp. Ideal for eating raw.

TOMATO TIPS

The hundreds of tomato cultivars vary in colour, size, shape, skin thickness, flesh density, pip size, juiciness and balance of sweetness to acidity. While each is a unique combination of features, they may be loosely grouped as beefsteak (large with dense flesh), plum, round, hollow (for stuffing), and cherry tomatoes.

Whatever the variety, the flavour will be better if it is ripened in the sun while still attached to the vine. Flavour is maximized if tomatoes are stored at room temperature, as refrigeration impairs both flavour and texture.

Yellow plum cocktail tomato

Small, plum-shaped tomatoes, with golden-yellow skin and paler yellow flesh. Juicy and sweeter-tasting than their red equivalent, they are best appreciated raw.

Cherry tomato

Small, bite-sized, round tomatoes. With a high sugar content, they are sweet and intensely flavoured, and are mostly eaten raw as a snack or in salads.

Eggplant/aubergine

A glossy, dark purple-skinned fruit with pithy, white, seeded flesh – the most common of the many varieties that come in varying shapes and colours. Popular in Mediterranean and Middle Eastern cuisines, it is baked, fried, grilled, pureed, stuffed and pickled. Initial salting helps to reduce its spongelike capacity to absorb oil.

Fuerte avocado

A pear-shaped fruit, with smooth, thin green skin and pale yellow-green flesh, mild in flavour, smooth and buttery in texture, encasing a large seed.

Hass avocado

A pear-shaped or oval fruit, with pebbly skin which changes from green to purple black when ripe. Its yellow creamy flesh, encasing a relatively small seed, has a smooth, buttery texture and mild, nutty flavour.

AVOCADOS

Avocados ripen off the tree, yielding at the stem end when ripe. They are eaten raw, most famously in guacamole; if cooked they become bitter. Because their flesh discolours rapidly once cut, they are best prepared at the last minute. Uniquely for fruit, they contain fat, with up to 25% monounsaturated fat.

SWEET PEPPERS

Sweet peppers, so called to distinguish them from the related but fiery chillies, are mild sweet fruits of *Capsicum annuum*. The term encompasses the variously coloured cube or bell-shaped bell peppers, which are also known as capsicums, the red heart-shaped pimientos, and some long, chilli-shaped varieties including the yellow to red tapering cubanelle, the yellow banana-shaped sweet banana peppers, and the pale-green curved bull's horn.

Chillies/chiles/chilli peppers

Certain fruits of the genus capsicum. The more than 200 varieties identified vary in size, shape, colour and taste and are known by different names in different places. Most ripen from green to shades of red, orange, yellow or brown. Their characteristic fieriness results from capsaicin, an alkaloid present mainly in the veins to which the seeds are attached; it is not water soluble. While fruits from the same bush can vary, in general the smaller the chilli the hotter it is; conversely, the broader its shoulders the milder it is; and the riper it is the sweeter and fruitier it is.

Green = unripe.
Yellow = Riper version.

Green and yellow bell peppers/capsicums

The bell-shaped fruit of *Capsicum annuum*; green peppers being
unripe, and yellow peppers a riper version. Green peppers have a
bittersweet flavour, their thick flesh being juicy and crisp when raw,
becoming more soft and mellow when cooked. They are prepared with
the seeds and membranes removed, variously sliced or diced, and
make a convenient container for stuffing.

Dried bird's-eye chillies

Small, thin, viciously fiery chillies, dried. Used
particularly in Thai cuisine, they are rarely deseeded.
They are often soaked in salted water before cooking,
or are grilled, or roasted, acquiring a smoky flavour,
before being ground.

Red bell peppers/capsicums

The ripe bell-shaped fruit of *Capsicum annuum*. They are commonly red or yellow (see
above), but also orange, purple, ivory and brown. With a mild fruity, sweet flavour, their thick
flesh is juicy and crisp when raw; when grilled or roasted, and their charred skins removed,
they soften and become sweeter. They are eaten raw. in salads and salsas, and cooked,
served as a vegetable, with pasta, in stews, sauces, and stuffed.

Pied Bleu/wood blewit

Mushrooms ranging in colour from lilac to violet to buff; the initially convex cap curls up to expose the gills. Their thick moist flesh is excellent to eat, but must be cooked to lose its mild toxicity.

Trompettes-des-Morts/horn of plenty

Greyish-black mushrooms with a soft funnel-like cap and virtually no gills. Not being very fleshy, they are fragile. Also delicate in taste, they are sautéed and used in sauces, sometimes to give an illusion of truffles.

Nameko

Tiny mushrooms distinguished by the slimy coating on their rounded amber-coloured caps and paler long curved stems. Extensively used in Japanese cooking, especially in miso soup, they have a gelatinous texture, and a light, aromatic flavour.

Girolles/chanterelles

Small mushrooms, shaped like a curved funnel with irregular, vein-like gills, and a colour and aroma of apricots. Edible raw, their relatively tough flesh tastes peppery. Cooked, they complement eggs.

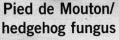

Pied de Mouton/ hedgehog fungus

Mushrooms distinguished by the spines pointing downwards from the underside of the yellowish cap. Fleshy and firm, they taste similar to chanterelles; their slight bitterness disappears on cooking.

Truffle

Fungal fruiting bodies which develop underground. Irregularly roundish, with solid, brittle white-veined flesh, they emit an intense permeating aroma. Black, or Périgord, truffles (depicted) with tough warty black skin, are usually cooked, peeled. Smooth beige White, or Alba, truffles are typically shaved raw over food, heat spoiling their more delicate flavour.

Porcini/cep/cèpe

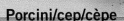

Prized mushrooms characterized by having tubes rather than gills under their burnished brown caps. Shaped like a champagne cork, with a delicate, musty aroma, their firm suc-culent white flesh is eaten raw, thinly sliced, and cooked, grilled and in stews.

Pom pom/lion's mane

Spherical mushrooms characterized by long, soft white spines and no stems. With a mild sweet flavour and a delicate texture compared to crab meat, it is generally gently cooked.

Oyster mushrooms/pleurote

Mushrooms shaped like a fluted oyster shell, ranging in colour from white to beige, pink or yellow. Their subtly flavoured, soft, succulent flesh is best cooked quickly. When larger, they are called 'abalone mushrooms.'

Portobello mushrooms

Large, flat, dark brown mushrooms with fully exposed gills; actually mature crimini mushrooms. They have a dense, meaty texture and concentrated flavour. Their size makes them suitable for grilling and roasting, whole.

Shiitake/golden oak/Chinese black

Umbrella-shaped mushrooms with brown caps fissured with white, and torn, cream gills. Of Japanese origin, they have an earthy fragrance, a meaty texture and a rich woodsy flavour. Best cooked, their tough stems first removed, they suit all cooking styles.

Dried chanterelles/girolles

Chanterelles/girolles mushrooms from which the moisture has been removed, leaving them dry, brittle and much reduced in size. Rehydrated, they retain their apricot colour but are rubbery in texture and relatively tasteless. The infused soaking liquid may be more useful.

Brown/crimini mushrooms

Umbrella-shaped mushrooms with a tan to dark brown cap. They have a deeper, earthier flavour than the closely related white mushroom. With firm flesh, they hold their shape well when cooked.

White mushrooms

Common white-capped mushrooms. At progressive stages of maturity, becoming denser in texture and stronger in flavour, they are: 'button' (depicted), closed around the stem and usually small; 'cup', the veil just begun to open around the stem; and 'flat', open with dark gills.

Fruit

In the botanical sense a 'fruit' is the structure of a plant, usually surrounding seeds, which develops from the flower ovary after pollination and fertilization. However, popular understanding of the term is based not on plant anatomy but on usage. Thus, in a culinary sense, a fruit is the edible part of a plant which is fleshy, succulent and sweet. Its sweetness, often balanced with acid, distinguishes 'fruit', in food terms, from other foods, notably vegetables. Some parts of a plant which technically are fruit are treated otherwise. Generally fruits are foods imbued with pleasure, and often eaten as the finale of a meal.

There are numerous species of fruit, from a variety of families. Many familiar fruits belong to two families in particular, Rose (*Rosaceae*) and Citrus (*Rutaceae*). Rather than botanical classification, fruits are commonly categorized by culinary characteristics: whether they have pips, stones, are berries, or soft. Fruits are also divided according to the season in which they ripen, and their place of origin.

Within species, different cultivars have been developed over the years for their individual attributes and habits.

Most fruits are suitable for eating raw, and some are well-suited to cooking. Many fruits can be preserved, often by drying, resulting in different eating and cooking properties.

Like fruit, 'nut' has a botanical definition that is rather more restricted than the popular sense of the term. Botanically, nuts are fruits, specifically one-seeded fruits, with a tough, dry outer layer. In common parlance a 'nut' is an edible kernel surrounded by a hard shell. Thus, fruit not technically nuts, such as almonds, and even non-fruit, such as peanuts, are treated as nuts.

Nuts generally contain little water, moderate protein, and much oil, predominantly unsaturated. Their high oil content renders nuts prone to rancidity, and to tainting by surrounding odours.

Often toasted to intensify their flavours, nuts are eaten as snacks and incorporated, whole, chopped or ground, into the sweet and savoury dishes of many cuisines.

Granny Smith

A variety of apple developed in Australia, round with greasy skin, bright green even when ripe, and juicy, crisp, tart, white flesh. It doubles as a dessert and cooking apple, readily collapsing to a puree when cooked.

Golden Delicious

A widely grown variety developed in USA. Elongated in shape, it has pale yellow-green skin and light, sweet, juicy flesh becoming sweeter and less crisp as it becomes golden. It is an all-purpose apple, excellent to eat and retaining its shape when cooked.

Red Delicious

The leading variety of American dessert apple. Distinguished by five knobs around its 'eye', it is large, elongated in shape, and has dark red, sometimes striped, skin. Its flesh is sweet and juicy but, as it lacks acid, can be insipid.

Pink Lady

A variety of Australian origin, a cross between Golden Delicious and Lady William (a Granny Smith cross). Its skin has a pink blush over a yellow background. With crisp, dense flesh and a tart-sweet flavour, it is an excellent dessert apple.

Red Williams

A red-skinned variety of the quick-ripening Williams pear, also
called Red Bartlett and Red Sensation. Its creamy white flesh
is sweet and very juicy with a buttery texture.
An excellent dessert pear, it is also good for cooking.

Doyenné du Comice

A large, squat variety of pear with a
speckled yellowish-green skin marked
with russet or blushed red; also known
as Comice. As a dessert pear it is
unrivalled: in texture its flesh is buttery
with no grittiness and very juicy; in
flavour it is sweet and aromatic.

RIPENING PEARS

Pears, their flesh surrounding a pip-
containing core, are pomes and are an
important tree fruit of temperate regions.
Unlike most fruit, pears are best picked
before they are ripe. They ripen from the
inside out and pass through their point of
perfect ripeness in a matter of hours.

Apricots

A rounded, fragrant temperate tree fruit of the rose family, with thin, velvety skin
ranging from pale yellow to deep orange, with soft, luscious yellow-orange flesh
encasing a large, rough, woody 'free' stone. They are eaten fresh, poached, roasted,
in tarts, stuffed and as jam. In Middle Eastern cookery they are much used in sweetmeats
and savoury dishes, especially with lamb. The kernels are used for their faintly bitter almond
flavour but, containing toxic prussic acid, should be roasted first.

Nectarines

A variety of peach, with smooth, fuzz-free skin, coloured yellow and red,
either 'freestone' or 'clingstone' according to the ease with which the
furrowed central stone separates from their yellow or white flesh.
Yielding, juicy and richly flavoured when tree-ripened, they are eaten fresh,
out of hand, poached or baked.

Plums

Temperate tree fruits of the rose family, with smooth, bloom-covered skins
and flesh-encased central stones. The many varieties range in shape from
round to oval, with skin and flesh colours from green to yellow, red and
purple, and in taste from acid to sweet. Categorized as dessert and cooking
plums, they are eaten fresh, out of hand, and poached, baked or preserved
as sauces and jam.

Peaches

Large, rounded, temperate tree fruits of the rose family, with downy skin
ranging from pink-blushed cream to red-blushed yellow, and pinkish-white or
orange-yellow flesh respectively. Like nectarines, they are either 'clingstone'
or 'freestone' according to the ease with which the flesh separates from the
stone. Soft, succulent and sweet when tree-ripened, they are eaten fresh, out
of hand and macerated, poached or baked.

Cherries

Small, round, temperate fruits of the rose family, with thin skins and flesh-
encased stones. Two main groups exist: sour cherries, subdivided into amarelle
(light coloured with clear juice) and griotte (dark with dark juice), eaten cooked;
and sweet cherries, ranging from white (actually yellow flushed with red) to
black (dark red to blackish), with firm, dry to soft, juicy flesh, a dessert fruit.
The intermediate sweet-sour category, either red or black, is often called 'Duke'.

White grapefruit

A large, round citrus fruit, descended from the pomelo, with yellow skin and yellowish-white flesh, seeded or seedless depending upon the cultivar. Assertively bitter in flavour, it is mostly eaten raw, either halved crosswise, its segments loosened, or segmented in salads. It is also cooked as marmalade, and its skin candied.

Lemon

An oval, subtropical citrus fruit, with yellow skin and paler flesh. Too sour to eat as a dessert fruit, it is an important culinary acidifying and flavouring agent. The acidic juice is used to enhance flavours, prevent discolouration, and counteract richness, while the zest is used for its aromatic essential oil, which is used as a flavouring.

Ruby grapefruit

A mutation of white grapefruit, with pink-blushed golden skin and seedless, ruby red flesh. Although bitter, it is sweeter than the white varieties.

BITTER TASTE

Grapefruit's bitter taste comes from naringin, a flavour compound that stimulates the taste buds. While naringin has beneficial properties, resulting in grapefruit having a reputation as a 'fat burning' fruit, it can also interfere with some digestive enzymes, affecting the body's metabolism and slowing the breakdown of certain medications.

Clementine

A tangerine cultivar (possibly a tangerine-sour orange cross). Small with thin, easily-peeled, orange-coloured skin it has red-orange, almost seedless, tangy-sweet flesh.

Navel orange

A large variety of sweet orange, with tight, easily peeled, pebbly, rich orange skin and a characteristic navel-like end. Richly flavoured and usually seedless, they are excellent for eating.

Tangerine/mandarin

A small citrus fruit, like a slightly flattened orange, with fragrant, loose orange skin and easily separable segments of sweet juicy flesh. In the UK, 'tangerine' denotes the lighter coloured, mild, seeded Mediterranean mandarin, whereas in the USA it means the darker common mandarin with a net of pith beneath the skin.

Lime

A small, tropical citrus fruit, with thin, fragrant, green or greenish-yellow skin and paler, juicy, very acidic flesh. Too sour for a dessert fruit, it is used as a culinary acidifying and flavouring agent. The true lime is the Mexican, West Indian or Key lime; the Tahitian or Persian lime is less lime-flavoured.

Minneola

Minneola is a variety of a tangelo, a tangerine-grapefruit hybrid. With a distinctive nipple at the stem end of smooth, deep-orange, easily-peeled skin, it has tart but sweet juicy flesh and few seeds.

Watermelon

A type of melon, of varying colours and proportions. Commonly, it is large and heavy, round or oblong, with a smooth rind of various green hues, and red or pink flesh studded with black seeds. Eaten fresh, its flesh, containing 90% water, is faintly sweet, insipid but refreshing. The rind is often pickled, or preserved in sugar syrup, and the seeds toasted and skinned to nibble as a snack.

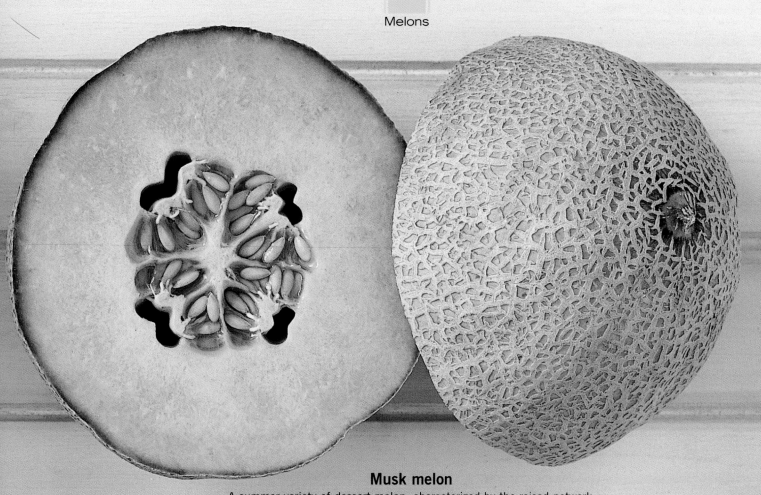

Musk melon

A summer variety of dessert melon, characterized by the raised network pattern overlaying the skin. When ripe, it is fragrant, the usually orange flesh very juicy and sweet. It is known by many names, including nutmeg, netted and sweet melon; rock melon in Australasia, and cantaloupe in North America. True cantaloupe melons are another variety of dessert melon and include Charantais, Galia and Ogen.

Honeydew melon

A winter variety of dessert melon; oval and lightly scented, it has relatively smooth, creamy-yellow, thick skin and pale green, juicy flesh.

GRAPES

The berries, borne in clusters, of vines of the genus *Vitis*. Small, rounded and plump, their smooth skins encase juicy pulp, which may contain up to four seeds. Grapes are classified by skin colour: white encompasses pale yellow-green to light green; black ranges from light red to purple-black. They are also distinguished by their use: dessert (also called eating or table grapes), juice, drying or wine. While all grapes are high in sugar, table grapes have relatively firm flesh and low acidity.

Of the approximately sixty species of grape, *Vitis vinifera*, grown in temperate regions, is the most widely cultivated. Some indigenous, cold-resistant North American species, notably *V. lambrusca*, the 'slip-skin grape', bear fruit with a musky, 'foxy' flavour.

SOME GRAPE VARIETIES

Thomson Seedless, also called Sultana is the most widely grown variety of table grape. Yellow-green, medium-sized, oval, thin-skinned and seedless, it is firm, juicy and very sweet.

Muscat denotes a group of varieties, white and black, with thick skins, and very sweet, aromatic, especially flavoursome flesh. Hanepoot meaning 'honey pot', also called Muscat of Alexandria, is a large, oval, yellow-green, seeded variety with firm, meaty pulp. Muscat Hamburgh, or Black Muscat, a large, oval, blue-black, and intensely flavoured grape is the second most widely grown variety.

Flame, a red, small to medium-sized, round, thin-skinned, seedless variety has firm, very sweet, juicy flesh.

Emperor is a red, large, elongated oval, thick-skinned, seeded, variety with a mild flavour.

Concord, a variety of *V. lambrusca*, found mainly in the USA, is bluish-black, large, seeded, and coarsely flavoured.

Red currants

Small, round, red berries with the withered remains of their originating flower on the end opposite the stem on which they cluster; their thin, shiny, often-translucent skin encases juicy, many-seeded flesh. They are a summer fruit, grown and appreciated mainly in northern temperate regions.
Tart and intensely flavoured, red currants are mostly eaten cooked, as preserves and in desserts such as Scandinavian fruit soup and British summer pudding.

Raspberries

Fruits of the rose family genus *Rubus*. The many individual, seed-containing fruits surround a conical core which remains on the cane when they are picked ripe. They have a slightly hairy surface and are usually red, but may be golden or white. Considered by many to be the supreme berry fruit, raspberries are velvety soft with an intense, sweet, slightly acid flavour. There are summer and autumn bearing varieties, both grown in cool climates.

Strawberries

The conically-shaped, glossy, fleshy, typically red 'false fruits' of the rose family genus *Fragaria*; botanically the strawberry is actually an enlarged receptacle on which the true fruits, the yellow seeds or 'achenes', are embedded. Wild or alpine strawberries are tiny, elongated and intensely flavoured, while the more common cultivated hybrid varieties are larger with a diluted flavour. Essentially summer fruits, strawberries are fragrant, juicy and flavoursome when picked fully ripe. They are mostly eaten raw, often with cream or sugar.

Cranberries

The rounded or oval shiny red fruits of the heather family genus *Vaccinium*, also called 'bounceberries' as they bounce when ripe. They grow wild in bogs and moors in northern Europe and North America, and are also commercially cultivated. Extremely tart, cranberries are made into sharp sauces and jellies to accompany game and, famously, turkey. Cranberry juice has a high concentration of vitamin C. Containing benzoic acid, and a natural preservative, they last well.

Cape gooseberry/Physalis
Not related to the gooseberry, these round, cherry-sized, yellow-green or golden-orange fruit are enclosed in a beige-coloured, inflated papery calyx or husk, resembling a Chinese lantern. The thin, waxy skin contains juicy, sweetly tart pulp with many tiny seeds. They are eaten raw, alone and in composite dishes, and cooked in desserts and jams. They are also called poha, golden berry and ground cherry.

Blackberries
Purplish-black fruits of the genus *Rubus*; the many individual seed-containing fruits surround a conical core which comes off the plant with the fruit, the whole eaten. The juicy berries are eaten both raw and cooked, the latter often teamed with apple. Wild blackberries are often called brambles.

Blueberries
Small, round, fleshy, cultivated fruit of the genus *Vaccinium*; their smooth skin, bluish-black with a silvery bloom, encases pale green or white flesh with insignificant seeds. Juicy with balanced acid /sweetness, they are eaten raw, or cooked in pies, muffins, jam and jelly.

Passion fruit

An egg-sized tropical fruit, also called granadilla; the hard, deep purple skin, slightly wrinkled when ripe, contains many small black seeds surrounded by viscous orange pulp. Fragrant, intensely flavoured and sweetly acidic, the pulp is eaten as is, and used, with or without the seeds, in desserts.

Pineapple

A cylindrical tropical fruit with a prickly, diamond-patterned green to gold skin, a crown of blue-green spiny leaves and juicy yellow, sweetly tart, fragrant flesh. Unable to ripen further, pineapples must be picked when ripe and aromatic. The 'eyes' and woody core are removed for eating, either raw or cooked. Raw pineapple contains bromelin, a protein-digesting enzyme.

Guava

A tropical fruit, varying in size, shape, and colour. All have a pulpy core, usually containing minute gritty seeds, encased by slightly granular flesh. Pervasively aromatic, acid but sweet, guavas are eaten fresh and preserved.

Papaya

A tropical, often pear-shaped fruit, also called pawpaw. Both the thin skin and the thick layer of flesh beneath ripen from pale green to yellow or reddish-orange. Unripe, papayas are eaten shredded in SE Asian salads or cooked as a vegetable. Ripe, the soft, sweet, delicately scented flesh is usually eaten raw, its lack of acid adjusted with lime juice. The peppery grey-black seeds packed in the central cavity, though edible, are usually discarded.

Banana
An elongated, curved, tropical fruit, varying in length. As it ripens the skin turns from green to red or, more commonly, yellow, then brown, and the encased firm cream flesh converts from starchy to very sweet, becoming soft and aromatic. Ripe, it is eaten raw or cooked; unripe bananas and non-sweetening varieties, called plantains, are cooked as vegetables.

Kiwi fruit
An oval, egg-sized fruit, formerly called Chinese gooseberry. Its light brown, hairy skin encases, commonly, bright green flesh with hundreds of tiny edible black seeds encircling a white core. Just giving when ripe, sweet and slightly acid, it is eaten raw. Extraordinarily rich in vitamin C, it also contains a protein-digesting enzyme.

Mango
A prized tropical fruit, variously round, oval or kidney shaped. When ripe its leathery skin shows shades of green and yellow, often blushed red. Surrounding a large, flat, fibrous stone, the orange or yellow, sometimes fibrous flesh is juicy and richly flavoured, with an acid-sweet balance and a resinous aroma.

Rambutan

An oval, tropical fruit, with red or yellow 'hairy' skin with soft spines. Within, the translucent, pearly-white flesh adheres to a narrow, shiny, brown seed with tough, papery skin. Closely related to the litchi, it is highly aromatic, firm and succulent, varying in sweetness and acidity.

Tamarillo

An egg-shaped, sub-tropical fruit of the nightshade family, formerly called tree tomato. Inside the smooth, thin, tough skin, variously orange to crimson, the succulent, strongly acidic orange or red flesh contains many small black seeds. Scooped out, it is eaten raw and cooked.

Custard apple

A sub-tropical fruit, also called cherimoya. It has thin, soft, pale green, inedible skin marked like scales and segmented, cream-coloured flesh embedded with large, hard, shiny black or brown seeds. Custard-like in texture, the flesh is sweet and delicately tropical in flavour.

Pomegranate

A large, roundish fruit with a hard, leathery, yellow to crimson skin. Numerous edible seeds surrounded by glistening, translucent, crimson pulp, are embedded in compartments of tough, tannic, yellowish membranes. Sweet yet tart, the juicy pulp is eaten as a dessert fruit, often sucked from the seeds, or used as a garnish.

Dates

The plump, fleshy fruit of the date palm. Fresh dates can be yellow, brown or red and typically contain 55% sugar. These oval or spherical fruits can be up to 7.5cm/3in long, with a narrow, grooved pip or seed.

Litchi/Lychee

A rounded, sub-tropical fruit, with thin, warty, leathery, pinkish-red skin. Its translucent pearly-white flesh encloses a large, shiny brown seed. Juicy, sweet, with a muscat-like flavour, the springy pulp is eaten fresh or lightly cooked.

Persimmon/kaki/sharon fruit

A sub-tropical, winter-ripening fruit, varying in colour, shape, size and astringency. Resembling tomatoes, with smooth, thin, shiny yellowish-orange to red skin, orange flesh and a large, dried green calyx. Astringent varieties contain tannin and must ripen to a jelly-like softness, their skins translucent, to be palatable; non-astringent or 'sweet' varieties, such as the seedless sharon fruit, are edible while firm. Other names include Japanese persimmon and oriental persimmon.

Figs

The fruit of the warm climate tree, *Ficus carica*. Inside the bulbous, vase-shaped, soft outer structure, is soft pink or purple flesh which contains hundreds of tiny seed-like fruits. Both skin and flesh are edible. There are four main types, with hundreds of varieties, classified by skin colour: white (which includes green), red and purple/black. Normally very sweet, figs are eaten raw, poached, baked or grilled.

Star fruit

A tropical fruit, star-shaped in cross-section, also called carambola, five corner and five fingers. With edible, waxy, translucent, yellow skin and crisp, juicy, yellow flesh it varies in sweetness and sourness by variety. It is eaten fresh, its ridges trimmed, or cooked.

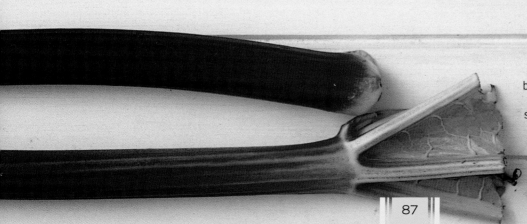

Rhubarb

Long, crisp, fleshy, red-shaded leaf-stalks, botanically a vegetable but treated as a fruit. Their intense acidity requires considerable sweetening. Often teamed with strawberries, ginger, orange or angelica, the stems are eaten cooked, especially in pies, hence the alternative name 'pie plant'. The leaves are toxic and are never eaten.

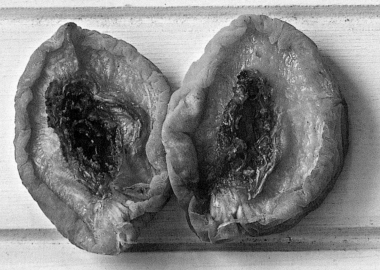

Prunes

Whole, sweet, free-stoned, dark-skinned plums, dried, and sold with or without pits. Sweet and chewy, with wrinkled black skins and amber flesh, prunes have a flavour distinct from plums. Modern succulent prunes are partially rehydrated.

Dried peaches

The dried flesh of unpeeled, halved, stoned peaches. Sweet and softly leathery, they have a mild peach flavour.

Dried dates

The partially dried, still plump whole fruits of the date palm. Sold pitted and unpitted, they have glossy, mahogany-coloured skin and firm, extremely sweet flesh.

DRIED FRUIT

Drying, the evaporation of natural moisture content, is one of the oldest known methods of food preservation. Traditionally food was dried in the sun; nowadays the more controllable method of forced hot air is also used.

In fruit, dehydration greatly concentrates flavour and sweetness, and alters texture. Vitamins A and C are depleted but other nutrients remain intact. The final moisture content ranges between 15 and 25 per cent.

To preserve the natural colour by preventing enzymatic browning, light-coloured fruits are often sprayed with a sulphur compound.

Dried fruits can be eaten as snacks, or used in baked goods, compotes and stuffings, and often reconstituted in water or alcohol (wine, brandy or other spirits).

Dried cranberries

The shrivelled, crimson, dried berries of the cranberry vine. With little natural sugar, they retain their fresh tartness. Sweetened dried cranberries can be used like raisins.

Dried mango

Strips or chunks of dried ripe mango flesh. The leathery, sugary fruit should be rehydrated before use. Reconstituted, it tastes and smells like fresh mango.

Dried apricots

The dried flesh of unpeeled, halved, stoned apricots. They are intensely sweet with a slightly caramelized flavour, yet an acidic tang, and softly leathery in texture. They are available fully dried or rehydrated for plump softness.

Dried figs

The whole fig, dried and compressed. Quite different in character from their fresh form, they are extremely sweet and softly chewy, their moist centres crunchy with seeds.

Dried apples

Dried rings of peeled, cored apple. Softly leathery, they are sweet with the underlying tartness of the fresh apple.

Dried sour figs

The dried, sweetly sour, pulpy fruits of a wild succulent, commonly called the fig-marigold, found around South Africa's Western Cape coast. They are typically used for jam, syrups and sweetmeats.

Dried pears

The dried flesh of unpeeled, halved, cored pears. Softly leathery, and less sweet than other dried fruits, they retain the subtle aromatic flavour of fresh pears.

Raisins

Dried whole grapes, shrivelled, dark in colour and very sweet. Traditionally made from sun-dried muscatel grapes with pips, nowadays raisins may be machine stoned, or made from seedless varieties.

Brazil nuts

A large, long, three-sided seed of an Amazonian jungle tree, encased in a triangular woody brown shell. High in mono-unsaturated oil, the brown-skinned, cream kernel has a tender texture and a rich mild flavour.

Hazelnuts

The fruit of temperate hazel trees. Small and round with a pointed tip, the brown-skinned, cream kernel is encased in a smooth, hard, brown shell. They are also called filbert and cob nuts, especially if cultivated.

Cashew nuts

A cream, kidney-shaped, tropical nut, with a sweet buttery flavour and a short texture. Always sold shelled, they are eaten out of hand and much used in Chinese and southern Indian cuisine.

Pecan nuts

The nut of a temperate hickory tree. With ridged grooves, the brown-skinned, beige kernel within its smooth tan oval shell resembles its walnut relative. The rich buttery kernels are high in monounsaturated oil.

Walnuts

The fruit of a temperate walnut tree. Encased in a round, brown shell, the brown-skinned, cream kernel is ridged and grooved like two halves of the brain. It is a versatile culinary nut, high in polyunsaturated oil.

Almonds

The kernel of the fruit of the temperate almond tree. Encased in a pitted beige shell, the flattish, pointed oval, cream kernel has a coarse brown skin, which is often removed (blanched). The sweet variety is delicately flavoured.

Macadamia nuts

The nut of a tree native to tropical NE Australia. Usually sold shelled, the smooth, spherical, skinless, creamy-white nut is high in monounsaturated oil, and rich and creamy.

Pistachio nuts

The kernel of the fruit of a native Asian tree. When ripe, the biscuit-coloured shell gapes, exposing the purplish skin covering the small all-green kernel. Mild, sometimes resinous in flavour, it is high in unsaturated oil.

Peanuts

A popular snack food in Western countries when roasted and salted, peanuts are a staple of Asia and Africa, used in satay sauces, curries and stews. (See also p60.)

Peanuts in shell

Not a true nut, peanuts are the seeds of a leguminous plant which develop underground, hence their alternative name, groundnuts. The shells, actually dried pods, are thin and brittle with a wrinkled surface network, but are easy to peel.

Coconut

The fruit of the tropical coconut palm, covered in a brown fibrous husk. When mature, the coconut has firm, white, fibrous flesh with thin, adherent brown skin encased in a hard shell. Coconut flesh is high in saturated fat.

Pulses
& Seeds

Seeds are the fertilized ovules of plants which, when sown, can produce a new generation of such plants. Those which contain a food store inside their protective coating are often a rich source of nutrition for humans.

Those termed 'seeds' in culinary parlance are more narrowly characterized; they are generally small, crunchy and mildly nut-like. Typically they are high in dietary fibre, minerals and oil, predominantly unsaturated, and contain moderate amounts of protein and small amounts of starch. Some are consumed as a food in their own right while others are used primarily as flavouring.

Pulses (legumes) are the edible seeds of leguminous plants, and so are borne in fleshy pods. While the term denotes both fresh and dried seeds, it is usually applied to dried peas, beans and lentils, and that is the state in which they are discussed in this chapter.

Of major importance to the human diet, pulses have been a staple since ancient times. They are excellent sources of protein, and contain the essential amino acid lysine, which is deficient in cereals. Thus pulses consumed in conjunction with cereals achieve a full complement of amino acids. They are rich in complex carbohydrates, B vitamins and some essential minerals. Unlike seeds, with some notable exceptions, pulses contain little fat.

Some pulses contain anti-nutritional properties and toxic substances, many of which can be denatured by proper cooking. The most notorious effect, however, is the propensity of pulses to cause flatulence: the oligosaccarides that are responsible are linked in a manner that human digestive enzymes cannot process, causing these sugars to reach the lower intestine unchanged, where they are metabolized by bacteria, giving off gases in the process.

Poppy seeds

The tiny dried seeds of *Papaver somniferum*, the opium poppy. (When harvested ripe, the seeds are not narcotic.) The variety most common in Europe is round, slate-blue, with a crunchy texture and a mildly nutty flavour. There it is sprinkled on top of breads and cakes, crushed and used as a pastry filling, and used to flavour potato and pasta dishes. The similar tasting, smaller, kidney-shaped, creamy-yellow seeds common in India are usually ground with spices and used to thicken and flavour sauces.

Sesame seeds

The small, flat, tear-shaped, waxy-looking seeds of the sesame plant. Ranging in colour, according to variety, from cream, the most common, to black, popular in Asia, they are mildly nutty, sweet and moderately crunchy, both taste and texture being more pronounced in black seeds. White sesame seeds are hulled. Primarily sprinkled whole over breads in European cooking, in Middle Eastern cuisine they are also ground to a paste (tahini), and compressed to make the sweetmeat halva. In China they are used as a crunchy coating for deep-fried food and in Japan as a condiment.

Sunflower seeds

The 'seeds', botanically fruits, of the sunflower. Typically encased in hard fawn and black striped shells, the edible beige kernels are small, flat and oval, with a pointed tip. To eat they are firm, slightly sweet and vaguely nutty. Popular as a snack food, raw or roasted, plain or salted, they are also added to breakfast cereals, baked goods and used in confectionery.

Pumpkin seeds

The seeds found inside a mature pumpkin. Creamy-white or brown shells encase flat, oval, dull green kernels. Firm with a subtle flavour, they are eaten as a snack food, both whole and hulled, raw, roasted and fried, and added to salads and baked goods. The hulled seeds, also called pepitas, are a traditional ingredient in Mexican cooking, ground to thicken sauces.

Hemp seeds

The edible, non-narcotic seeds of the plant *Cannabis sativa*. Rich in essential fatty acids and essential amino acids in an easily digestible form, they are mainly consumed for their health and nutritional qualities. They have a nutty taste, akin to sunflower seeds, and can be similarly used. Outlawed in some countries, they are used as a food in Poland, Russia and Japan.

ROASTING SEEDS

Roasting seeds accentuates their flavour. If they are not to be otherwise cooked, recipes often call for them to be browned (toasted) before use. Heating should be gentle and careful, as their high oil content causes seeds to burn readily.

As seeds contain significant percentages of oil, predominantly unsaturated, they are prone to rancidity. In order to delay their deterioration they should be stored in an airtight container in a cool, dark place.

Pine kernels

The seeds of various species of pine tree, the most prized being from the Mediterranean Stone Pine, also called piñon, pinyon, and pignolia. Extracted from between the pine cone scales, they are small, ivory, and shaped like a triangular teardrop. In texture they are relatively soft and slightly mealy, in flavour delicate and faintly resinous. Used in sweet and savoury dishes, especially in Middle Eastern and Mediterranean cuisine.

Haricot/navy beans

Small, white, oval beans. Cooked, they are smooth in texture and, though bland, absorb flavours well. These versatile beans are commonly used for baked beans.

Red kidney beans

Characteristically kidney-shaped beans, with dark red skins and cream-coloured flesh. Full flavoured and mealy, they are much used in Mexican cooking.

Borlotti/cranberry beans

Large kidney-shaped beans with magenta-speckled beige skins, which become uniformly brown when cooked. They have a creamy texture and ham-like flavour.

Black (Mexican) beans

Shiny black-skinned beans with a strong, smoky, mushroomy flavour and smooth texture. Also called turtle beans, they are popular in Latin America and Spain.

Butter beans

A large flattish, fine-skinned, white variety of lima beans, also called Madagascar beans. With their buttery flavour and smooth texture, they are often puréed.

Adzuki (azuki) beans

Tiny, russet beans with a sweetish flavour, also called red bean. Popular in Asian, especially Japanese, cooking, they are used mainly in sweet dishes.

Flageolet

Young haricot beans, small and kidney-shaped with tender, pale green skin. Delicately flavoured, they are a classic French accompaniment to roast lamb.

Ful medames

A small, rounded brown variety of broad bean. Also called Egyptian brown beans, they are an Egyptian staple, used for the popular traditional dish of the same name.

Broad/fava beans

Large, flat beans, with tough green, beige or brown skins, also called faba, Windsor, field and horse beans. Cooked, they are creamy, with a mealy texture. The strong flavour improves if first skinned.

Cannellini beans
Large, white, kidney-shaped beans, with squared-off ends. Popular in Italy, cooked, they are mild in flavour and fluffy in texture. Rounded Great Northern beans are often sold as cannellini.

Black-eyed beans
Small, cream-skinned beans with a black spot, also called black-eyed peas or cow peas. Mildly flavoured, they are a feature of the 'soul food' of the southern USA.

Mung beans/green gram
Tiny, olive-skinned beans with yellow interiors. Used whole, they need no soaking, cook quickly, are slightly sweet and easily digestible.

Soya bean
Small oval beans varying in colour from yellow to brown and black. An excellent source of protein, and a staple food in much of SE Asia.

PREPARING DRIED BEANS

All dried beans, except mung beans, require soaking before they are cooked. There are two methods of soaking, each with advantages. 'Slow soaked' beans are immersed in water for several hours, usually overnight; they rehydrate better, but unless they are kept cool there is a risk they will begin to ferment. 'Quick soaked' beans are first boiled for five minutes, then soaked, covered, for two hours; this is much faster but, because they do not rehydrate as well, they are more likely to disintegrate when cooked. For both methods soak the beans in three times their volume of water.

To improve digestibility, discard the soaking water and use fresh water for cooking. Some recipes advocate the addition of an alkalizer, such as baking soda, to hasten cooking. However, this destroys nutrients. Do not add acidic ingredients or salt until the beans are tender, as these will prevent further softening.

Certain beans, notably lima and kidney, contain natural cyanogens, which metabolize to form the gas hydrogen cyanide, which can inhibit breathing. It is destroyed by boiling, but leave the pot uncovered to allow the gas to escape.

Split green peas
Dried green peas, with their outer skins removed, split in half. They do not require pre-soaking and disintegrate in cooking. Mildly earthy in flavour, in European cooking they are most widely used in thick soups, particularly teamed with ham, while in India they are a type of dal (which means split pulse), called mattar dal, and are used in dal, the purée.

Split yellow peas
Dried yellow peas, with their outer skins removed, split in half. As with split green peas, they do not require pre-soaking and disintegrate in cooking. Split yellow and green peas are used in much the same way (see above) and can be made from either garden or field peas.

Whole dried peas
Dried mature whole peas, with slightly wrinkled, dull blue-green skins, also called blue peas. They require long soaking and tend to cook to a mealy textured mush. Traditionally they are made into thick soups and pease pudding. In England boiled mushy peas are a popular accompaniment to fish and chips. Roasted and spiced, they are an Indian snack food.

Puy lentils

Tiny leguminous seeds, dark green with blue marbling, grown in Puy in the Auvergne region of France. When cooked they retain their shape and become brown. Considered to have the best texture and flavour of lentils, Lentilles vertes de Puy are a relatively expensive delicacy.

Chickpeas

Rounded, beaked legumes with furrowed, thick, fawn skins. Generally eaten dried, they are extremely hard so need preliminary soaking. Nutty flavoured and mealy textured, they are much used in Spanish, Middle Eastern and Indian cooking, notably puréed in hummus and ground in falafel. They are also called garbanzo beans and Bengal gram.

Brown lentils

The small, round, bi-convex dried seeds of a leguminous plant. Sold whole, with their greenish-brown skins intact, they are also called green or continental lentils. They retain their shape when cooked and are often used in hearty dishes combined with pork.

Red lentils

The small, round, bi-convex dried seeds of a leguminous plant. Sold skinned and split, they are salmony-orange in colour and cook quickly to a yellow purée. Also called Egyptian lentils and masoor dal, they have a spicy flavour and are used for soups and dal.

Dairy

Dairy pertains to milk and its derivatives. Milk is an opaque white fluid secreted by female mammals. Intended as the sole sustenance for newly born offspring it is very nutritious. 'Milk', without qualification, generally denotes cow's milk. However the milk of many other mammals is also a source of human food.

A complex structure, milk is an emulsion, suspension and solution of fat globules, protein, salts, sugar and vitamins in water. While most milks contain the same substances, they vary in their proportions from species to species, and within the same species, according to breed.

When fresh milk stands, the fat globules, being too large to remain in suspension and lighter than water, eventually rise to the top, forming a rich layer, called cream. Creaming, the separation of milk fat, is now usually achieved by centrifuge.

By its nature, raw milk is hospitable to microbes and is readily tainted. Many milk-based products derive from measures to control this susceptibility and some exploit it to advantage.

Thus, the conversion by certain bacteria of lactose to lactic acid gave rise to yoghurt and sour cream. Nowadays, routine pasteurization, the combination of high temperature and time, destroys most of the microbes, both harmful and beneficial, in raw milk.

Much milk is also homogenized, a treatment forcing milk through tiny holes. Broken thereby into smaller globules, the fat is distributed through the milk and cannot 'cream'.

An egg is a spheroidal reproductive body, laid by a female animal. Containing the potential embryo and, importantly, its food reserves, enclosed in a shell or membrane, eggs are extremely nutritious. All eggs consist of a thick, viscous, transparent liquid 'white' surrounding a round sac of opaque yellowish 'yolk'. The white is composed of mostly water and some protein; the yolk of protein, water and fat.

Being porous, egg shells are pervious to odours, water and air. At the large end of an egg is an air pocket, which enlarges as the egg ages. The freshness, or otherwise, of an egg can thus be tested by whether it contains sufficient air to float.

Full-cream cow's milk

Milk whose composition is as it emerged from the cow. Also called whole milk, it contains on average 3.9% butterfat (cream). It may or may not be homogenized.

Low-fat cow's milk

Milk from which typically half of the original butterfat (cream) has been centrifugally removed, leaving a fat content of 2%. It is paler and thinner than whole milk. Also called semi-skimmed or 2% milk.

Fat-free cow's milk

Milk with a fat content of below 0.15%, virtually all of the butterfat (cream) having been centrifugally removed. Also called skimmed milk, it is relatively pale and watery.

Goat's milk

A very white milk. Apart from containing no folate, it has a similar composition to cow's milk, with marginally less sugar and protein and an average of 4.1% fat.

Powdered milk

Milk evaporated, usually by spray-drying, until almost all its water is removed. Low fat milk is preferred because fats quickly oxidize, affecting flavour. Also called dried milk, it keeps for months if cool and airtight. It is used as is in baked goods, or reconstituted.

Evaporated milk

Milk concentrated by evaporating up to 60% of its original water, then homogenized, canned and heat sterilized. Thick, with a cooked, caramel flavour, it is used, as is, as a cream substitute or diluted as whole milk (in desserts and baked goods). Unopened, it keeps indefinitely.

Condensed milk

Milk concentrated by evaporating up to 60% of its original water, then sweetened with sugar and canned. Preserved by its high sugar content, it keeps well. Intensely sweet, thick and sticky, it is used in desserts, baked goods and confectionery.

Buttermilk

Originally the liquid remaining after ripened cream had been churned to butter. Nowadays skim milk is slightly fermented with special cultures to make cultured buttermilk. Low in fat, mildly sour and thick, but pourable, it is drunk and used in pancakes and baked goods.

Pouring/single cream

Cream with a butterfat content of at least 18%. Called single cream in the UK and light cream in the USA, it is used as a pouring cream, and will not whip.

Thickened cream

A pourable cream with a butterfat content of 35% to which a small amount of thickening agent, such as gelatin, rennin or alginate, has been added. Whipped, it maintains a larger volume with less likelihood of separation.

Thick double cream

A heavily homogenized, spoonable cream with a minimum butterfat content of 48%. Thick double cream is not pourable and cannot be whipped, unlike double cream and heavy whipping cream (see below).

Sour cream

Pasteurized, homogenized single/light (18% fat) cream soured by a lactic acid-producing culture which thickens it and imparts a piquant tang. Stabilizers are sometimes added. If boiled, sour cream will curdle.

Crème fraîche

Cultured French fresh cream, actually lightly fermented high butterfat cream. Thick, rich and distinctively tangy, much used in French cuisine; it boils without curdling, and offsets sweetness in desserts.

Smetana

A thick, rich mixture of sour and fresh double cream, milder in taste than sour cream alone, much used in Russian, Central and Eastern European cuisine. As the souring is caused by bacterial fermentation, smetana normally has a short shelf-life.

CREAM: GRADES AND FAT CONTENT

It is the fat content of cream which determines both its richness and its capabilities: the more fat cream contains the richer it is, the less likely it is to curdle when heated and, to an extent, the more readily it whips (see below). Accordingly, cream is graded by its fat content. The precise contents of the grades, and their labels, vary by country.

Percentages stated are minimum amounts of butterfat.

- Half cream, also called Top of the Milk (UK) is 12% fat; Half and Half (USA) is 10.5%. It is intermediate between milk and cream, and cannot be whipped.
- Single (pouring) and Light cream (USA), at least 18%.
- Medium cream (USA) is 25%.

- Whipping cream (UK) and Pure cream (Australia) is 35%; Light whipping cream (USA) ranges from 30–36%.
- Heavy whipping cream (USA) ranges from 36–40%.
- Double cream (UK), and Rich cream (Australia) is 48%
- Clotted or scalded cream (UK) is the thickest of all, at 55%. It is spoonable only.

To whip, cream needs a fat content of at least 20% (between 30 and 40% is ideal). This produces a light foam double its original volume. Beyond 40% whipped cream more readily becomes lumpy and buttery.

Salted butter
Sweet or lactic butter with varying amounts of salt added. As well as acting as a preservative, salt adds flavour. This is the most common type used for spreading, as salted butter burns more readily.

Unsalted butter
Sweet or lactic butter with no salt added. Having no preservatives, it is more perishable than salted butter. Containing less sediment, it is less likely to burn, so is preferred for cooking, and is ideal for sweet recipes.

Farm butter
Traditionally made, often by hand, on farms where cream is produced. Using unpasteurized, naturally ripened cream, its tangy, full, nuanced flavour differs from farm to farm.

Ghee
The Indian version of clarified butter. Melted butter, its fat separated from its solids, is simmered until the water evaporates and the solids turn brown. Ghee has a nutty taste, keeps well and has a high smoke point.

SWEET & LACTIC BUTTER

Made by churning cream until the fat coalesces into a semi-solid state, butter is a water-in-oil emulsion consisting of 80% fat, 2% milk solids and 18% water. It hardens when cooled and melts when warmed. Butter made from unripened cream is termed sweet cream butter, while that made from cream ripened by lactic acid-producing bacteria is termed lactic, cultivated, ripened or cultured butter.

The traditional butter of continental Europe, lactic butter, is gently tangy and fuller in flavour than its sweet counterpart, prevalent in the UK and USA.

Butter is used as a spread, a flavoursome ingredient and a cooking medium. It has a relatively low smoke point, the milks solids precipitating and burning. To avoid this butter is clarified by heating then skimming off the solids.

Flavoured butter
Butter creamed with herbs, spices, sweet or savoury flavourings (here, garlic and parsley). Used as spreads, sliced cold on grilled meats and vegetables, as toppings for baked potato or whisked into sauces .

Plain/natural yoghurt
Whole or skimmed milk fermented and coagulated by lactic acid-producing bacteria. High fat versions are more stable when cooked. Smooth in texture, with an astringent, sour taste, it has varied uses.

Strained/Greek yoghurt
Yoghurt strained of its whey, traditionally made by hanging to drip in a muslin cloth, until it is very thick and creamy in texture. Suitable for use in desserts, or sweet or savoury dishes. High in fat.

Soy milk
A milk-like liquid made by boiling soaked ground soya beans in water, then filtering it. Used as a dairy milk substitute; often fortified with calcium.

Powdered soy milk
Soy milk evaporated until almost all its water is removed, leaving the solids in powder form. It must be reconstituted with water before use.

Powdered rice milk
Evaporated version of a non-dairy, milk-like liquid made by straining the liquor off cooked rice ground with water.

NON-DAIRY MILK
The milk sugar, lactose, makes milk difficult to digest; indeed many adults, particularly Asians, cannot digest it at all. However, in the process of transforming milk into yoghurt or cheese, bacteria convert lactose to lactic acid, making a more digestible product. Foods such as yoghurt, soy and rice milk are often easier to digest, thus their nutritional benefits become more available.

Soybeans are also indigestible if eaten whole, and most of their protein passes straight through the digestive system. Their extraction as milk renders their protein digestible.

Ostrich egg

The enormous egg of the ostrich, a large bird indigenous to Africa. The largest of all eggs, ostrich eggs weigh on average 1.5kg/3.25 lbs, the equivalent of 24 hen's eggs. Their pale shells are necessarily strong, so hard to crack. With a pronounced eggy flavour, they are excellent for cooking, best used for baking, and are sometimes dried.

Goose eggs

Varying in size, but typically equivalent in volume to three hen's eggs. They have robust, hard-to-crack white shells and a very strong flavour. Best suited to cooking, they are renowned for making outstanding cakes. Often laid in dirty places, they should be used very fresh and long-cooked to kill bacteria.

Hen's eggs

The eggs of domestic chickens are the commonest eggs and what is meant by the unqualified term 'egg'. The shells range from white to brown, according to breed, their colour not indicating the egg's taste.

Sold by size, eggs are classified in the EU from size 1 (70g/2½oz plus) to size 7 (45g/1½oz or under) and in the USA from jumbo to peewee. Most recipes are based on an average 60g/2oz egg (UK size 3 or 4; Large in USA).

Thousand year eggs

Duck eggs preserved by coating with a paste of lime, wood ash and salt then covering them for six weeks, also called hundred year and century eggs. The amber, jellied whites and green, creamy yolks, are mildly sulphurous and blue cheese-like in taste. Typically served cold and shelled as an appetiser, with pickled ginger.

Quail's eggs

Small, about a third the size of a hen's egg, they have relatively large, dense yolks and watery whites. Their brown-speckled greenish-beige shells have a thick inner membrane which makes neat peeling difficult. Delicate in flavour, they are often served hard-boiled, sometimes in aspic, or used as a garnish.

Cheese

Cheese is, essentially, a mass of solids extracted from curdled milk. It is, however, phenomenally diverse in character, the result of the many variations in the extraction process. Cheeses range in taste from mild to strong, in aroma from imperceptible to pungent, in texture from soft to hard, in colour from white to yellow to blue, in size from tiny to huge, in fat content from low to high, and in age from fresh to mature, all with nuances in-between.

Because of the many variables, there is no single standard cheese-making method; nevertheless, all cheeses have certain processes in common. First the milk is soured, and thereby separated into curds (solids) and whey (liquid). Next the solids are concentrated: a coagulant, often rennet, is added and/or the curd is 'cut', and sometimes 'cooked', then drained of whey; some are also pressed. Finally the formed cheese is variously ripened: some from the outside, either by the growth of a white mould or surface bacteria; others internally by their original starter bacteria.

The amount of moisture left in the curds, and the related fineness of the particles, determines the type of cheese; moist cheeses, generally being more susceptible to bacteria, ripen faster. Hard cheeses, which have much of their moisture removed, take longer to mature.

The type of milk used also influences the character of the cheese. The differing compositions of milk from different species and breeds, whether it is skimmed, whole or enriched, and whether it is raw or pasteurized, all contribute to flavour, colour and texture in cheese.

The place where the cheese is made also makes a difference. The animal's diet, often geographically specific, plus indigenous air-borne moulds, impart unique qualities to cheese. Many cheeses are named for their place of making.

The significance of these variables has been recognized by the award of Protected Designation of Origin (DOP) and *Appellation d'Origine Contrôlée* (AOC) status to certain cheeses.

Their diversity of styles and tastes makes classifying cheeses difficult. As well as milk type and origin, they are frequently grouped by the nature of their rind and their overall texture.

OTHER TRADITIONAL ENGLISH WHITE CHEESES

Lancashire is a white semi-firm cheese made by combining the curd of raw or pasteurized cow's milk from three different days. As the curds ripen at different rates, it has a mottled texture and mild flavour. Moist and creamy when young, maturing to crumbly, it melts well and is ideal for making Welsh rabbit.

Wensleydale is a hard-pressed cheese made from whole pasteurized cow's milk. Eaten young, the white version is tangy, moist and crumbly.

White Stilton is made from pasteurized cow's milk, to the same recipe as blue Stilton but omitting the mould. It has a crumbly texture and a mild, slightly acidic flavour.

Cheddar

A hard cheese, made from whole cow's milk, raw or pasteurized. Traditionally large, drum-shaped and clothbound, and matured for one to five years, it has a complex, nutty, tangy, lingering flavour, and a firm, creamy texture. Originally named for its Somerset (UK) village of origin, it is the most famous of English cheeses, and widely copied.

Cheshire

An English hard cheese, made from whole cow's milk, raw or pasteurized. Naturally creamy, with a moist, crumbly texture, it is slightly acidic, salty, and mild in flavour.

Red Leicester

An English hard cheese, made from raw, whole cow's milk. Coloured russet by annatto, it is flaky, with a mild flavour. An easy grating cheese, it melts well and is ideal for Welsh rabbit.

Derby

An English hard cheese, made from pasteurized, whole cow's milk. Cheddar-like but softer and flakier, it has a mellow, buttery flavour.

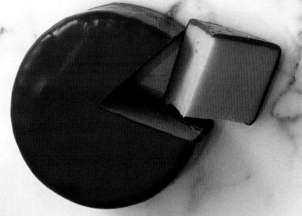

Caerphilly

A Welsh hard cheese, made from whole cow's milk, raw or pasteurized. Ripe in days, the whitish, moist, crumbly interior has a mild acid tang.

Double Gloucester

An English hard cheese, made from rich, partially ripened, raw cow's milk. Coloured orange, it is smooth with a mellow, savoury flavour. When locally sold, it has a natural rind.

Leiden/Leyden

A Dutch hard, washed-curd cheese, made with semi-skimmed, pasteurized cow's milk. Its creamy, nutty curd is spiced with cumin or caraway seeds.

Havarti

A Danish semi-soft cheese, made from pasteurized cow's milk. With small irregular holes, it has a spongy texture and a creamy full flavour, becoming pungent with age.

Maasdam

A Dutch, semi-soft cheese, made from pasteurized cow's milk. Supple, with largish Emmenthal-like holes, it has a mellow, sweet, nutty flavour.

Gouda

Dutch washed-curd cheese, made from whole cow's milk, raw or pasteurized. Smooth, elastic, with small holes, its mild buttery flavour matures to tangy complexity.

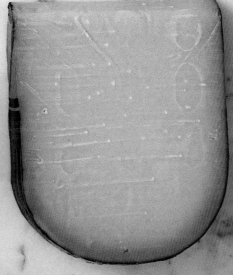

Boerenkaas

Literally 'farmer's cheese', boerenkaas is usually gouda made on the farm from raw cow's milk.

Edam

A Dutch, semi-soft, washed-curd cheese, made from semi-skimmed pasteurized cow's milk. Ball-shaped, with a smooth, rubbery texture, its bland flavour sharpens with age.

Old Amsterdam

A Dutch Gouda-type cheese, made from pasteurized cow's milk, and aged for 18 months. It is moist and firm with a full, nutty flavour.

Monterey Jack

A Californian semi-soft cheese, made from pasteurized cow's milk, whole or skimmed, also called 'California Jack' or 'Jack'. Moist, smooth and bland when young, it is firmer and sharper when aged or 'dry'.

Emmenthal

A Swiss cooked, hard cheese, made from raw cow's milk. Formed in large wheels with a dry natural rind, it is matured for four to 18 months. The yellow interior is evenly punctuated with smooth hazelnut-sized 'eyes' and has a sweet, fruity tang.

Smoked Montgomery

Cheddar made traditionally by Montgomery's in Somerset, England, then oak-smoked. The smokiness overlays the full nutty flavour of this brown-tinged cheese.

Fontina

A unique Italian semi-soft cheese with DOP status, made in Val d'Aosta from whole, raw cow's milk. The concave wheels are matured for three months. Scattered with tiny eyes the dense, smooth, straw-coloured curd has an earthy character.

Comté

A French cooked, hard cheese with AOC status, made from raw cow's milk, also called *Gruyère de Comté*. The convex-sided wheels are aged for three months. Dotted with cherry-sized eyes, the interior has a firm, supple, granular texture and a salty, fruity, nutty tang.

Cantal

A hard, cow's milk, AOC cheese from France, also called *Fourme du Cantal*. Initially springy and sweet, it ages to firm and strongly flavoured.

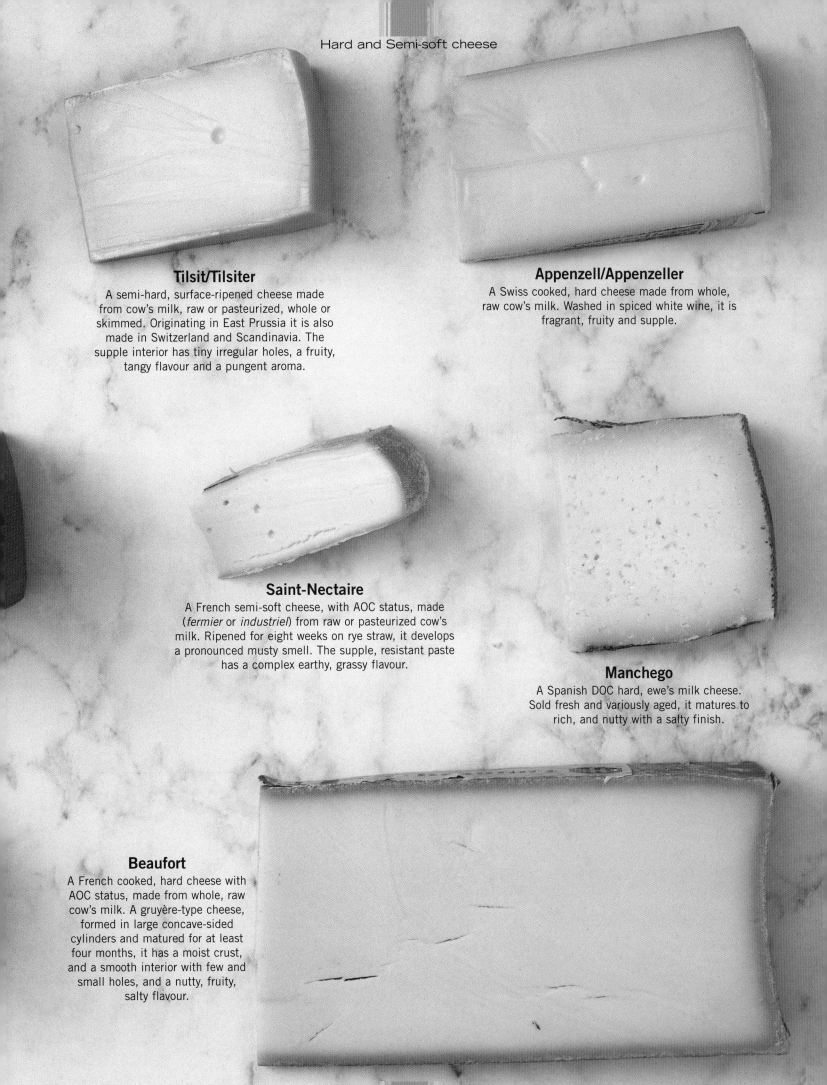

Tilsit/Tilsiter

A semi-hard, surface-ripened cheese made from cow's milk, raw or pasteurized, whole or skimmed. Originating in East Prussia it is also made in Switzerland and Scandinavia. The supple interior has tiny irregular holes, a fruity, tangy flavour and a pungent aroma.

Appenzell/Appenzeller

A Swiss cooked, hard cheese made from whole, raw cow's milk. Washed in spiced white wine, it is fragrant, fruity and supple.

Saint-Nectaire

A French semi-soft cheese, with AOC status, made (*fermier* or *industriel*) from raw or pasteurized cow's milk. Ripened for eight weeks on rye straw, it develops a pronounced musty smell. The supple, resistant paste has a complex earthy, grassy flavour.

Manchego

A Spanish DOC hard, ewe's milk cheese. Sold fresh and variously aged, it matures to rich, and nutty with a salty finish.

Beaufort

A French cooked, hard cheese with AOC status, made from whole, raw cow's milk. A gruyère-type cheese, formed in large concave-sided cylinders and matured for at least four months, it has a moist crust, and a smooth interior with few and small holes, and a nutty, fruity, salty flavour.

Parmigiano Reggiano

A hard, cooked, Italian *grana* (grainy) cheese with DOP status, made from raw, partially skimmed and ripened cow's milk. Formed in huge cylinders, with the maker's marks branded on the convex sides, it is matured for at least one and up to four years. It has a brittle, crumbly, granular texture, with crunchy crystals of calcium lactate, and an intense, complex, fruity, sharp flavour. Known as parmesan in English, it is principally shaved or grated as a seasoning.

Grana Padano

A hard, cooked Italian cheese with DOP status, made from raw, partially skimmed cow's milk. Produced and aged like Parmigiano Reggiano, it has a flaky, grainy texture and mellow to piquant taste.

Pecorino Romano

Italian cheeses made from ewe's milk. The hard, cooked types, some with DOP status, have salty, granular interior, initially moist and elastic, becoming dry, firm, sharp and intensely flavoured with age. They are eaten as a table cheese and, when matured between eight and twelve months, are used grated, as a condiment. Pecorino Romano, from Lazio and Sardinia, is the best-known version.

Asiago

Two Italian cow's milk cheeses with DOP status: Asiago d'Allevo, made from raw, skimmed milk, is matured for a year or more, the initially mild interior becoming hard, grainy and slightly sharp in flavour; Asiago Pressato, made from whole, pasteurized milk, is springy with deep irregular eyes and eaten young, when mild and milky in flavour.

Gruyère

A Swiss hard, cooked cheese, made from raw cow's milk. Formed in medium-sized wheels, it is long matured, typically ten to twelve months. It is dense, with far apart, pea-sized holes and has a robust, complex, nutty flavour. It is favoured for cooking.

MOZZARELLA AND OTHER STRETCHED-CURD CHEESES

Stretched-curd (*pasta filata*) cheeses, with their characteristic elastic texture, are so-called because the cut curd is put into hot water until it forms a plasticized mass then, while still hot, stretched, and either kneaded or spun.

Porcelain-white, mozzarella is composed of multiple thin layers with droplets of whey trapped within. Best within a few days of making, it is eaten both as a table cheese and cooked, famously atop pizza. Its elastic texture becomes more so when melted.

Traditionally, mozzarella is made with whole milk from the water buffalo, and *Mozzarella di Bufala* has DOP status. Considered to be the finest version, buffalo mozzarella is subtly sweet, mossy, rich and lactic. Nowadays, mozzarella is more widely made from pasteurized cow's milk, and sometimes called *fior di latte* to distinguish it from buffalo mozzarella.

Buffalo mozzarella
Buffalo mozzarella is a soft, fresh, Italian stretched-curd cheese, spun into balls and briefly immersed in brine. It is sold bathed in whey. Bocconcini are small balls of buffalo mozzarella.

Provolone

A stretched-curd cheese, traditional in Southern Italy, made from whole, pasteurized cow's milk. Shaped in various formats, it is eaten young, aged and smoked: *dolce*, aged two to three months, has a thin rind and firm, supple, smooth, delicately flavoured curd, becoming stringy when cooked; *piccante*, from six to 24 months, has a tough rind and flaky interior with a stronger, tangy flavour.

Caciocavallo

A stretched-curd, cheese, traditional in Southern Italy, usually made from pasteurized cow's milk. Shaped like a gourd, it is hung to dry. When young, it is sweet, elastic and mild and eaten as a table cheese. Matured up to two years it becomes piquant and granular and is grated as a condiment.

Porcini brie

A soft creamy cheese with a central layer of porcini (see p68). The mushrooms enhance the natural fungal flavour of the cheese. (See also p122.)

Explorateur

A French soft, white-rind, triple-cream cheese, factory-made from pasteurized cow's milk. Matured for three weeks, it is firm, rich and creamy.

Ricotta

An Italian fresh whey cheese, made from raw cow's, goat's or ewe's milk. The snowy-white mound of fine, moist grains is sweet, milky and mild.

Mascarpone

An Italian thick soft, acid-coagulated cream, made from cow's milk. Containing up to 40 per cent fat, it is rich and sweet.

Cream cheese

Firm, spreadable unripened cheese made from pasteurized cow's cream; sometimes also milk. It is smooth and mildly tangy.

FRESH CHEESE VARIANTS

- Quark (quarg), a soft, unripened curd cheese made from skimmed cow's milk. Sold in pots, it is smooth and lightly sour.
- *Fromage Frais* (fresh cheese) and *Fromage Blanc* (white cheese), are unripened cheeses made from cow's, goat's or ewe's milk. With a high moisture content and mousse-like texture, they are mild with a lemony zing.

Within individual cheese types fat contents vary:
- Standard cream cheese contains at least 33% fat; low-fat or light cream cheese has half that and non-fat cream cheese no fat at all. Commercial cream cheese may contain a stabilizer.
- Fromage frais ranges from *maigre* (5%) to triple crème (75%).
- Quark with some fat restored is called *Speisequark* and with cream mixed in is *Rahmfrischekäse*.

Creamed cottage cheese
Cottage cheese enriched by the addition of four to eight per cent cream.

Cottage cheese
A fresh spreadable cheese made by draining acid-curdled cow's milk, usually skimmed. The snowy-white moist mass of lumpy curds, of varying size and density, has little flavour.
Sweet-curd cottage cheese, popular in America, is washed to remove acidity.
Large curd varieties are also called 'popcorn cheese'.

Labneh/Labna
A Lebanese fresh cheese. Made by straining the whey from raw cow's or ewe's milk yoghurt, the curd ranges from soft and creamy to firm and rollable.

Paneer/Panir
An Indian cheese made from whole, pasteurized cow or buffalo milk. The acid-curdled milk is strained, and the remaining curd pressed until firm. Soft unpressed paneer is called 'chenna'.

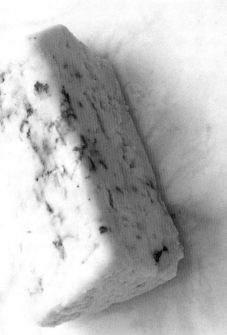

Bleu d'Auvergne

A French blue cheese with AOC status, made from raw and pasteurized whole cow's milk. Originally an imitation of Roquefort made with cow's milk, its moist, sticky, creamy interior is evenly veined with blue-grey mould. It has a strong smell and sharp, spicy, integrally salty taste.

Roquefort

A unique French blue cheese with AOC status, made from raw or pasteurized whole ewe's milk. To qualify, the fresh cheeses, inoculated with *Penicillium roqueforti*, must be ripened in the humid, mould-ridden, natural limestone caves of Combalou, in SW France, for at least three months. Initially pale and green, the mould becomes bluer, then grey as the cheese ripens and small blue-grey holes form in the ivory interior. It has an open creamy moist texture, and a piercing, rich, spicy, salty flavour.

Bleu de Bresse

A French small, brie-style blue cheese, made from pasteurized cow's milk. Pockets of blue-grey mould, sometimes surrounded by the fluffy white mould which also coats the rind, dot the dense, moist interior. Rich and creamy in texture, it is relatively mild in taste.

BLUE-VEINED CHEESE

Blue cheese is so-called for the blue or green mould which veins the body of the cheese. Originally accidental, nowadays the coagulated curd is inoculated with a specific penicillin mould. Because the mould only grows and blues when exposed to air, blue cheeses are never pressed and, in many cases, the curd is pierced to admit air. In cheeses too dense for the mould to spread it is inoculated directly into the young cheese. Traditionally, blue cheeses are matured in humid cellars where the bacteria continue to work.

Stilton

An English blue cheese, made from pasteurized whole cow's milk. Of protected legal status, it is made only in Leicestershire, Nottinghamshire and Derbyshire. Formed in tall, straight-sided cylinders, matured for four to six months, it has a crusty rind and yellow interior evenly spread with jagged veins of blue mould. It is creamy, rich and tangy.

Gorgonzola

An Italian blue, uncooked cheese, with DOP status, made from whole cow's milk. Traditionally a mix of two raw milk curds, and ripened in caves, nowadays most is made with pasteurized milk, and matured in storerooms for three to six months. Its straw-coloured interior is marbled with greenish-blue veins of its own *Penicillium glaucum* mould. Especially creamy in consistency, in flavour it contrasts delicate richness with sharpness.

Dolcelatte

An Italian blue cheese, factory-made from whole cow's milk. Aged for two to three months, grey-green mould splotches the straw-white interior. It is soft and creamy with a delicate, mellow flavour; the name literally means 'sweet milk'. It is a mild version of Gorgonzola and is also called Gorgonzola dolce (sweet Gorgonzola).

Camembert

A French soft, white-rind cheese. Widely copied, true AOC camembert is made in Normandy from raw cow's milk in 250g/9oz wheels measuring 10cm/4in across. Ripened three to six weeks it becomes supple and custard-like in consistency with mushroomy flavours, the rind stippled reddish.

Port-Salut

A French semi-soft washed-rind cheese. Originally made by Trappist monks, it is now factory-made from pasteurized, usually whole, cow's milk. Ripened for a month, the 25cm/10in diameter wheel has a slightly moist orange crust. The pale orange interior, sticky when cut, is pliable and smooth textured, with a mild taste and faint aroma.

Brie

A French soft, white-rind cheese. Much imitated, true brie is made in Ile-de-France from raw, whole cow's milk, in large discs. Ripened, its downy rind reddens and its chalky interior becomes almost runny, with a creamy, mushroomy taste.

Boursault

A French soft, white-rind, double-cream cheese, named for its creator and also called Lucullus. Factory-made from pasteurized cow's milk enriched with cream, it is creamy yet solid with a mild, nutty, buttery flavour, its slight acidity balancing the richness.

Munster/Muenster

A French semi-soft, washed-rind cheese, with AOC status, made in Alsace from whole, raw or pasteurized cow's milk. With an orange rind and pungent smell, it has a smooth, supple textured, sweet yet savoury, spicy flavoured interior. A smaller version, made in Lorraine, is called Géromé.

Livarot

A French semi-soft, washed-rind cheese, with AOC status, made in Normandy from raw or pasteurized, partly skimmed cow's milk. It has a pungent aroma, a dense, supple texture and an assertive, earthy flavour.

Taleggio

An Italian semi-soft, washed-rind cheese, with DOP status, made from raw or pasteurized cow's milk. Formed in 20cm/8in square slabs, it has a thin pinkish bloomy rind and a smooth, supple, straw-white interior with only a few eyes. Those ripened for 25–40 days in the caves of Valsassina, near Como, have a pronounced aroma and a fruity, buttery taste.

Pont l'Evêque

A French semi-soft, washed-rind cheese with AOC status, made from whole, raw or pasteurized cow's milk. Formed in ridged squares, matured two to six weeks, it has an ochre rind, a glistening, springy, open interior, an earthy aroma, and a piquant, sweet tang.

Romadur

A German semi-soft, washed-rind cheese, factory-made from cow's milk. Formed in small rectangles or cubes and matured three to four weeks, it has an ochre to reddish rind and an assertive smell and taste.

Feta

A Greek fresh, white 'pickled' cheese. Traditionally made from whole, raw ewe's milk, nowadays most is factory-made from pasteurized cow's and goat's milks. Formed in rindless blocks, then cured and stored in whey, brine or oil, it is soft, crumbly, rich, sharp and salty.

Halloumi/Haloumi

A Cypriot fresh, stretched-curd cheese, traditionally made from raw ewe's milk, sometimes with a layer of mint leaves. Stored in brine, the blocks of elastic, fibrous curd have a salty, mild, milky taste. It is principally cooked, holding its shape when heated.

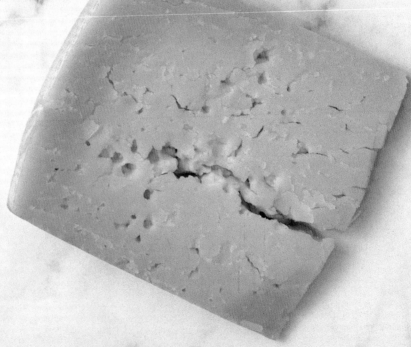

Kefalotyri/Kefalotiri

A Greek hard cheese, made from whole, raw ewe's or goat's milk. Named for the brimless hat it resembles in size and shape, it is white to pale yellow with many irregular holes. Sharp and slightly salty, it is used as a table cheese when young, and cooked and grated when older.

Banon

A French soft, natural rind cheese, made from raw ewe's, goat's or cow's milk. The small disks are wrapped in wine-steeped chestnut leaves tied with raffia to mature for two to eight weeks. Nutty and lactic when young, it becomes sharp, vegetal, and strong-smelling with age.

Rocamadour

A French soft, natural rind cheese with AOC status, made from raw goat's or ewe's milk. It is also called Cabécou de Rocamadour. The small thin disks of 30–60g/1–2oz mature rapidly, developing a thin, wrinkled rind and a smooth creamy interior with a fresh acid taste, becoming firmer and nuttier with age.

NATURAL RIND CHEESES

Natural rind cheeses are allowed to develop their own crust from the various moulds and wild yeasts that progressively colonize their wet, protein-rich surface. Initially tufts of fuzzy white penicillin appear, then patches of delicate blue mould, followed by grey, yellow and eventually red, the cheese shrinking and wrinkling as the ripening proceeds.

Crottin de Chavignol

A French natural rind cheese with AOC status, made from whole, raw goat's milk in the shape of a small flattened ball. Over four months it progresses from pure white, a soft, moist grainy texture and a fresh, lemony flavour, to a deeply wrinkled, hard black rind with a hard, sharp, robustly flavoured interior.

Meat

'Meat' nowadays denotes the flesh of animals used as food. Exactly which animals and which flesh are included in this usage is ambiguous. Fish is certainly not, and whether poultry is considered 'meat' depends on the context; it is often distinguished from meat in the sense of 'red meat', and in this book is treated in a separate chapter. Offal (variety meats) too is sometimes excluded, but is included here.

The animals most commonly consumed as meat are cattle (oxen), sheep and pigs; they have long been domesticated and bred for this purpose. Game, be it wild or, as latterly, farmed, is eaten to a lesser extent.

While all meat has characteristics in common, from a consumer's point of view the meats of individual species have different qualities, influenced by their breed, age, sex, diet, level of activity and manner of slaughter.

For the cook, the cut of meat is also significant. Butchery, however, is fraught with confusion. The way an animal is jointed varies from country to country, even from region to region, according to the nationally preferred methods of cooking, and also evolves with food fashion. This complexity is compounded by the various, often overlapping, names given to similar cuts.

Key to understanding the virtues of the various cuts of meat is an appreciation of which part of the animal they are from and their function. Those muscles which had the most exercise, generally the forequarter and the lower part, develop the coarsest fibres and tend to be the toughest, with a correspondingly full flavour. Fat, particularly intramuscular fat, called marbling, also contributes to tenderness and flavour; during cooking it melts and penetrates the tissue, separating and lubricating the fibres. Bones also add flavour, as well as conduct heat.

These factors determine the most appropriate method of cooking: tender meat suits hot, dry modes; tougher meat is better suited to slow, moist cooking which dissolves the collagen in the connective tissue surrounding the muscle fibres.

Hump

A boneless forequarter cut from the hump on the back of the
neck of cattle deriving from the hot-climate *indicus* species.
With a coarse texture and abundant intramuscular fat, it is
suitable for pot roasting and corning whole, cutting into
stewing steak and grinding into mince.

Neck

A forequarter beef cut from the upper part
of the neck behind the head, adjacent to the
chuck. Relatively lean and one of the least
tender and flavoursome cuts, neck is usually
cut up as stewing steak and sometimes ground
or minced. The neck and its adjacent cuts are
sometimes also known as clod or sticking.

Bolo

A boneless forequarter beef cut from the upper shin
and lower chuck, consisting of several separable
muscle layers running in different directions. It has a
coarse texture and very little intramuscular fat. It is
pot roasted whole, thinly sliced for minute steaks,
cubed for stews, and minced (ground).

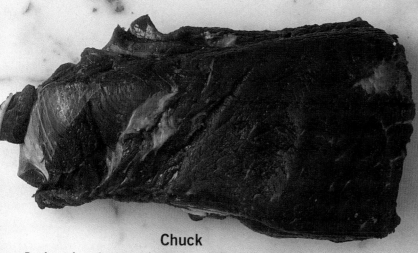

Chuck

Beef cut from between the neck and shoulder blade, beneath the blade meat. Sold boned in the UK and with the bone-in in the USA, it is well-marbled.

Standing rib (on bone)

A forequarter beef cut of the ribs between the wing ribs and chuck. Also called fore rib, it is a traditional lean, tender roasting joint on the bone. Boned and rolled, it becomes rolled rib roast.

Flat rib/thin rib

Beef cut from between the fore rib and brisket. With two thin layers of muscle separated by connective tissue and fat, it is often boned and rolled.

Shin

The lower part of the, traditionally fore, legs, also called shank. Usually sold sawn into horizontal slices, lean, tough muscle with a lot of connective tissue surrounds the central bone. When cooked, necessarily long and slowly, it is flavoursome, rich and gelatinous.

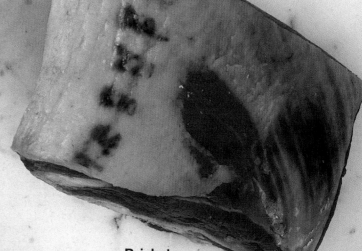

Brisket

A forequarter beef cut from the breast or lower part of the shoulder. It can be divided into the point and the plate or flat end. Sold bone-in, boned and rolled, and often corned (cured), it is best slowly cooked, pot roasted, braised or boiled. It is fatty with a good flavour.

Thin flank

A boneless hindquarter beef cut, from the underside of the rump and loin, which includes the skirt steak. Fatty, gristly and fibrous, it is frequently minced. Cut into pieces it may be stewed; whole, it may be salted or pickled and boiled.

Beef fillet

The long, tapering, boneless 'eye' cut from the centre of the sirloin. Extremely lean and tender, though lacking flavour, it is roasted whole or sliced into steaks, variously tournedos, filet mignon, fillet steak and chateaubriand, for grilling and frying.

Wing rib

A forequarter cut of beef, consisting of rib bones with the sirloin attached, positioned to the rear of the fore rib on the carcase. With a uniform covering of fat and lean meat, it is an excellent joint for roasting.

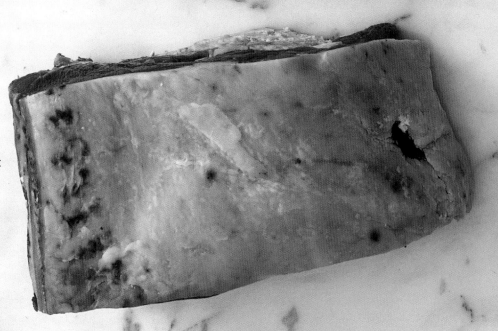

Sirloin

A hindquarter beef cut from the back between the ribs and rump (the shortloin and round in the USA). The attached fillet may be removed. Very tender, with a good layer of fat, it is excellent for roasting. It is sold both on the bone and deboned and rolled, or sliced into steaks including entrecôte, porterhouse and T-bone.

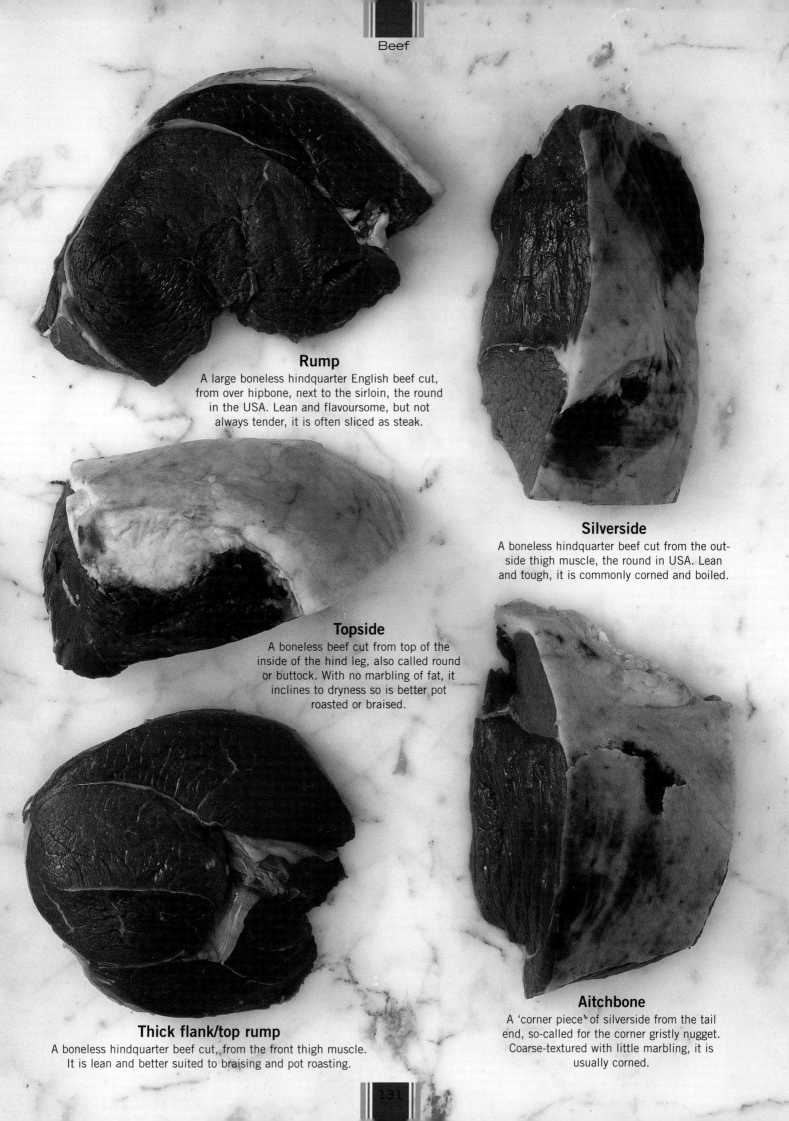

Rump

A large boneless hindquarter English beef cut, from over hipbone, next to the sirloin, the round in the USA. Lean and flavoursome, but not always tender, it is often sliced as steak.

Silverside

A boneless hindquarter beef cut from the outside thigh muscle, the round in USA. Lean and tough, it is commonly corned and boiled.

Topside

A boneless beef cut from top of the inside of the hind leg, also called round or buttock. With no marbling of fat, it inclines to dryness so is better pot roasted or braised.

Aitchbone

A 'corner piece' of silverside from the tail end, so-called for the corner gristly nugget. Coarse-textured with little marbling, it is usually corned.

Thick flank/top rump

A boneless hindquarter beef cut, from the front thigh muscle. It is lean and better suited to braising and pot roasting.

Beef sausage

A generic term for fresh beef which has been coarsely or finely chopped, or minced (ground), seasoned, and sometimes mixed with cereal binder, then stuffed into casings, traditionally lengths of animal intestines. Typically made from lesser cuts, sausages usually contain considerable fat. Before eating, fresh sausages must be cooked, either boiled, baked, fried or grilled.

Beef strips

Thin strips of boneless beef muscle, cut across the grain. Because they are typically quickly cooked over a high heat, they should be from a tender joint, such as rump, and uniform in size and thickness so that they all will cook in the same time. Strips are used in dishes such as beef Stroganoff and commonly in Chinese and stir-fry recipes.

Beef cubes
Chunks of boneless beef muscle. Usually cooked by long slow moist methods, they are cut from less tender joints with more connective tissue, such as chuck, blade, shin and flank. Variously stewed, braised and casseroled they become tender, while remaining intact, and have rich flavour.

Beef mince
Raw beef which has been finely chopped or minced (ground), also called ground beef and hamburger. While any meat can be minced, less tender cuts, or their trimmings, are usually used, with the quality and fat content varying accordingly. Mince is versatile and can be used for hamburger patties, pasta sauce, meatballs and stuffings.

Whole sucking pig

A young pig, fed only on its mother's milk, slaughtered when between two and six weeks old. A traditional feast food, it is roasted, often on a spit, and served whole, classically with a small red apple in its mouth. Its meat is pale, tender and gelatinous and, in a contrast of textures, its skin makes excellent crackling.

Belly

A thin cut of pork with thin layers of fat and muscle in equal proportion, sold bone-in and boned and rolled.

Pork fillet/tenderloin

A long cylindrical boneless pork cut, from the hindloin beneath the backbone. Lean and tender, it is cooked whole, sliced into medallions and diced, variously roasted, pan-fried, and grilled.

Hand and spring

A cut of pork consisting of the shoulder of the foreleg, the hand, with part of the belly, or spring, attached. It is suitable for roasting, boiling and especially stewing and braising, the skin, bones and connective tissue imparting a viscous quality.

Spare ribs

The long rib bones removed in one piece from a pig's belly, an American and Chinese cut, not to be confused with the British 'spare rib' cut from the shoulder. Fatty, with meagre meat, they are usually separated, marinated, then roasted or barbecued and the meat gnawed from the bones.

Loin

A cut from the middle of the pig, spanning the backbone, with the belly removed. Sold on the bone and boned and rolled, it is also cut down further into fore and hind loin, and various chops and steaks. It is a prime roasting joint.

Chump

A hindquarter pork joint, cut from the full leg at the rump end and including the pelvic bone; with the bone removed, it is called the rump. Roasted whole, it can also be cut into meaty chops for frying and grilling.

Pork leg
The hind leg of the pig, with the trotter removed, called 'fresh ham' in USA. A large joint, it is often cut into two: the meatier top part is called the fillet end and chump end; the lower portion is called the knuckle half and short leg. Sold bone-in, or boned and rolled, it is usually roasted.

Trotter
The foot of the pig. Bony and sinewy, it requires an initial long, slow cooking to soften. It may then be boned, stuffed and braised, roasted, or grilled. It makes a flavoursome, gelatinous stock, so is used to enrich stews and to make brawn.

Knuckle/shank
The lower portion of the pig's leg or shoulder, cut immediately above the trotter, also called hock. It is sold fresh, salted or smoked. With the skin on and bone in it makes a gelatinous stock, and is commonly braised.

Diced pork

Cubes or chunks of boneless pork. Usually cooked by long, slow, moist methods, cubes are cut from less tender joints, such as the shoulder.

Pork mince

Raw pork which has been finely chopped or minced (ground). Usually less tender cuts, such as hock, shoulder or trimmings, are used, the quality and fat content varying accordingly. Pork mince is especially used for terrines and forcemeats.

Pork schnitzel

A large, thin slice of pork. Cut across the grain, typically from the leg and loin, and usually beaten to make thinner. Commonly it is pan-fried, sometimes crumbed, or rolled around a stuffing.

Gammon

An English term for the hind leg of a pig, usually the upper part, cured as for bacon and sold uncooked. Being more lightly cured and requiring cooking, it differs from ham. It is sold in joints, for roasting, as well as moderately thick steaks and rashers.

Chipolatas

A small pork sausage, half the size of a regular sausage. Authentic English chipolatas are a mix of seasoned lean and fat pork and ground rice stuffed into sheep's intestines and linked into short lengths. They are a traditional garnish for roasted poultry.

GRADING LAMB AND MUTTON

Sheep meat is graded according to age: lamb is younger than 12 months; from one year, when the animal gets two incisor teeth it becomes hogget or two-tooth; from two years, when it has four teeth, it becomes mutton. In the UK the distinction between hogget and mutton is not made, and sheep meat is known as mutton from one year on.

Whole lamb

The carcass of a young sheep, with the head, tail and innards removed. Typically roasted on a spit, and served whole, it is a festive dish. Milk-fed baby lamb, slaughtered when three to four weeks old, weighing 4–5kg (9–11 lb), is suited to such cooking. Called house lamb in the UK, it has very pale, tender flesh, but lacks flavour.

Middle neck

A forequarter sheep cut, from the upper shoulder between the scrag end and best end of neck, also called Spanish neck. It is often cut into chops. Bony with a lot of fat, it is best cooked slowly and gently.

Breast

A forequarter cut, on the bone, from the belly of the sheep. Because it is fatty it is often boned, trimmed and rolled, then roasted or braised.

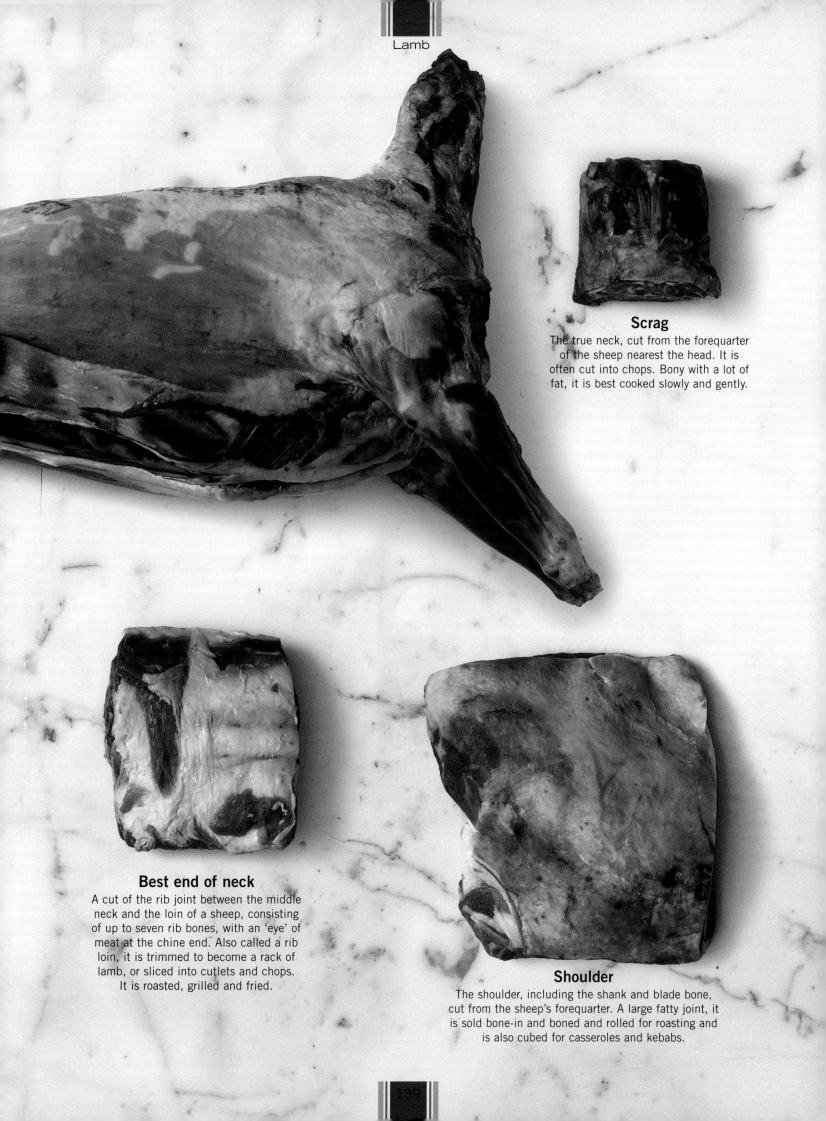

Scrag

The true neck, cut from the forequarter of the sheep nearest the head. It is often cut into chops. Bony with a lot of fat, it is best cooked slowly and gently.

Best end of neck

A cut of the rib joint between the middle neck and the loin of a sheep, consisting of up to seven rib bones, with an 'eye' of meat at the chine end. Also called a rib loin, it is trimmed to become a rack of lamb, or sliced into cutlets and chops. It is roasted, grilled and fried.

Shoulder

The shoulder, including the shank and blade bone, cut from the sheep's forequarter. A large fatty joint, it is sold bone-in and boned and rolled for roasting and is also cubed for casseroles and kebabs.

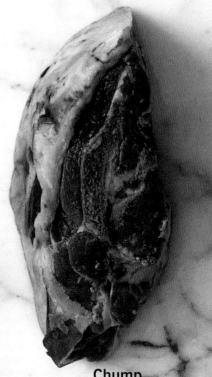

Chump

A bony hind cut from the rear end of the loin above the leg, also called rump. It is sold whole and cut into chops.

Loin

A cut from either side of the backbone extending from the ribs to the chump, also called the mid-loin. Whole, on or off the bone, it is roasted; sliced into chops, it is grilled and fried.

Noisette

The tender eye of the loin, or the rack of lamb, completely boned out, then rolled and tied around, usually with an outer layer of fat.

Saddle of lamb

Two loins, or mid-loins, connected by the backbone and some-times including the kidneys, also called a double loin. Tender with a good covering of fat, it makes a grand roasting joint.

Striploin

A flattish, boneless strip cut from the loin, or mid-loin. Lean and tender, it is cooked whole or sliced across the grain. Beneath the striploin is the fillet (not shown), a small, lean, tender boneless strip cut from along the backbone.

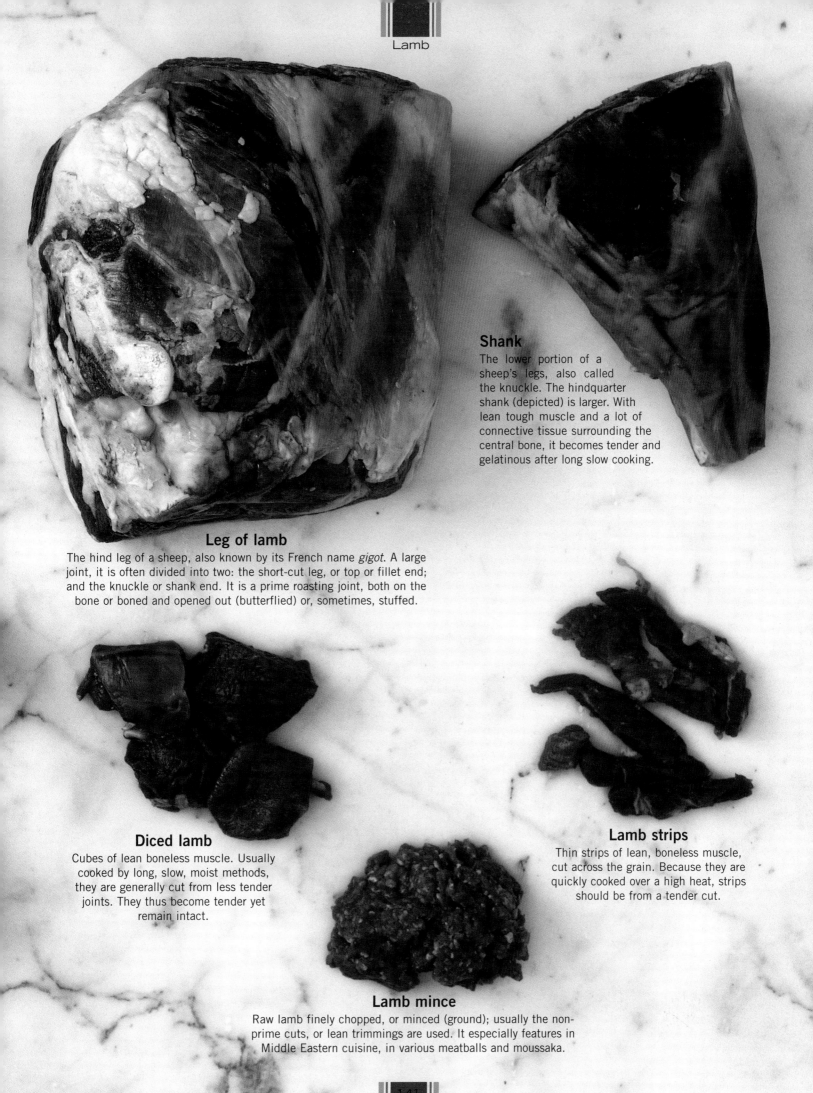

Shank

The lower portion of a sheep's legs, also called the knuckle. The hindquarter shank (depicted) is larger. With lean tough muscle and a lot of connective tissue surrounding the central bone, it becomes tender and gelatinous after long slow cooking.

Leg of lamb

The hind leg of a sheep, also known by its French name *gigot*. A large joint, it is often divided into two: the short-cut leg, or top or fillet end; and the knuckle or shank end. It is a prime roasting joint, both on the bone or boned and opened out (butterflied) or, sometimes, stuffed.

Diced lamb

Cubes of lean boneless muscle. Usually cooked by long, slow, moist methods, they are generally cut from less tender joints. They thus become tender yet remain intact.

Lamb strips

Thin strips of lean, boneless muscle, cut across the grain. Because they are quickly cooked over a high heat, strips should be from a tender cut.

Lamb mince

Raw lamb finely chopped, or minced (ground); usually the non-prime cuts, or lean trimmings are used. It especially features in Middle Eastern cuisine, in various meatballs and moussaka.

Veal loin
A hindquarter veal cut, from between the ribs or best end and rump. Whole, often boned and rolled, it is a prime roasting joint.

Rump
A boneless hindquarter veal cut, from between the loin and the leg. Whole, it is roasted or braised.

Loin chop
A slice of the veal loin, also called a veal cutlet. Typically it is fried or grilled, sometimes crumbed.

Leg
A hindquarter veal cut, comprising the leg fillet, silverside and topside, usually divided into smaller cuts. It is especially lean and tender.

Veal shank
The bony lower portion of the calf's hind leg, also called the knuckle. The gelatinous tissue surrounding the marrow-rich bone is sawn into rounds for the Italian classic osso bucco.

Schnitzel
A large thin slice of veal cut across the grain from the upper leg and beaten to make it thinner. Coated with egg and breadcrumbs, then pan-fried it becomes the Viennese classic Wiener schnitzel.

Escalope
A thin, boneless, round or oval slice of veal cut across the grain from the upper leg. Marginally thicker than schnitzel, it is usually pan-fried.

Kangaroo fillet

The undercut of the loin of an Australian marsupial. Lean and tender, it is best cooked briefly at a high temperature.

Wild boar

A single loin, depicted on the bone, of the sometimes-farmed wild boar. The meat is darker and leaner than conventional pork, with a more pronounced, gamey flavour, and is usually marinated.

Crocodile fillet

The boneless flesh from the tail of a farmed saltwater crocodile. It is lean, with a texture akin to fish and a chicken-like taste.

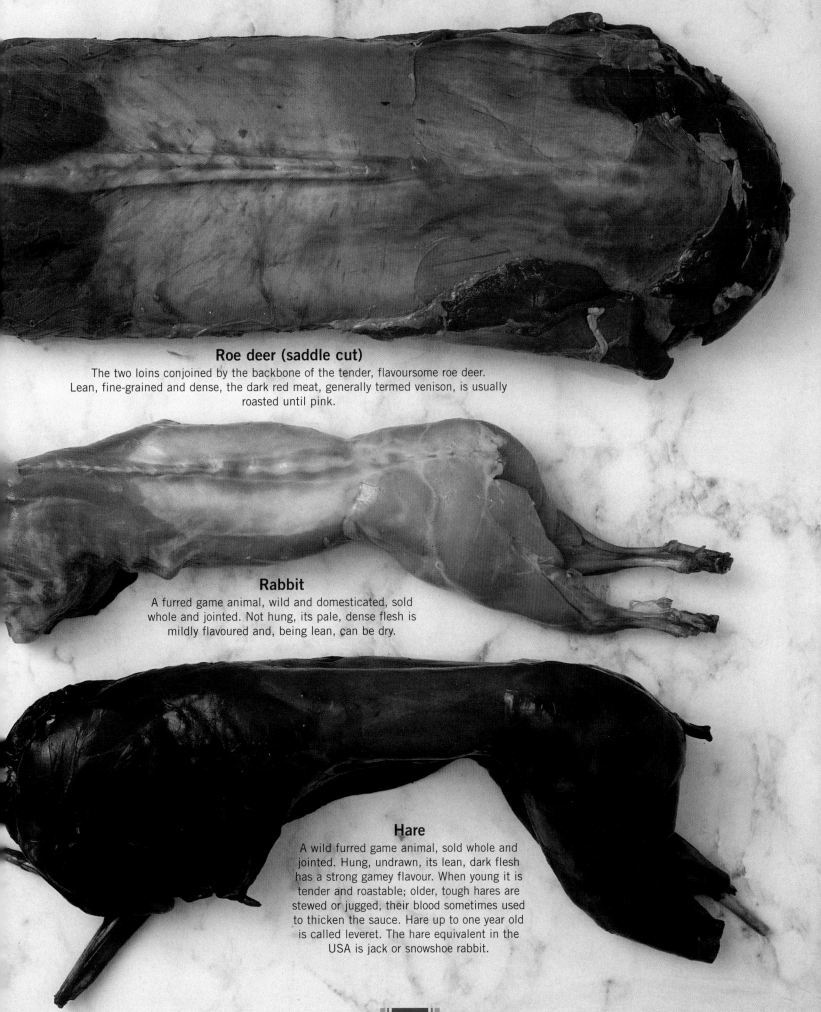

Roe deer (saddle cut)
The two loins conjoined by the backbone of the tender, flavoursome roe deer.
Lean, fine-grained and dense, the dark red meat, generally termed venison, is usually
roasted until pink.

Rabbit
A furred game animal, wild and domesticated, sold
whole and jointed. Not hung, its pale, dense flesh is
mildly flavoured and, being lean, can be dry.

Hare
A wild furred game animal, sold whole and
jointed. Hung, undrawn, its lean, dark flesh
has a strong gamey flavour. When young it is
tender and roastable; older, tough hares are
stewed or jugged, their blood sometimes used
to thicken the sauce. Hare up to one year old
is called leveret. The hare equivalent in the
USA is jack or snowshoe rabbit.

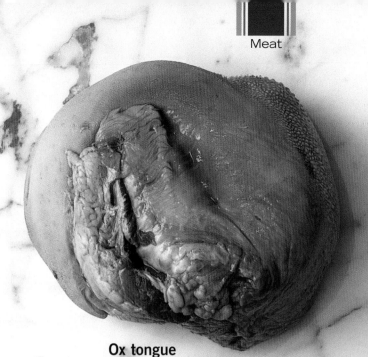

Ox tail
The skinned tail of an ox, usually sliced across the central bone. Slowly cooked in soups and stews, it is gelatinous but can be fatty.

Ox tongue
The tongue of an ox, sold fresh or cured. Stripped of the tough skin after prolonged moist cooking, it is eaten hot or cold.

Ox kidney
A large multi-lobed ox's organ, here with its surrounding suet, membrane and core removed. The strong flavour can be muted by soaking and prolonged cooking.

Tripe
The lining of one of an ox's first three stomachs, each distinguished by its texture. Usually sold processed, it requires lengthy cooking.

Lamb's liver
The blood-purifying organ of a sheep. With the covering membrane removed, and cooked until just pink in the middle, it is tender and full flavoured. In Australasia, lamb's liver is also called lamb's fry.

Heart

An organ consisting mostly of muscle. Trimmed of excess fat and piping, and usually stuffed and braised, it is dense, fibrous and full flavoured.

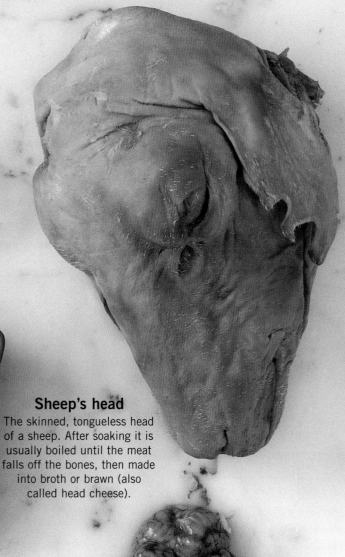

Sheep's head

The skinned, tongueless head of a sheep. After soaking it is usually boiled until the meat falls off the bones, then made into broth or brawn (also called head cheese).

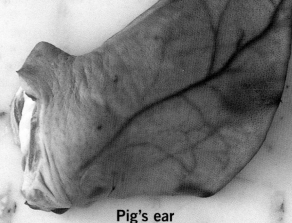

Pig's ear

Cartilaginous meat, washed and singed, softened by lengthy simmering, then typically crisply finished by breadcrumbing and baking or frying.

Lamb's brain

Pale meat, convoluted in form. Initially soaked, blanched and the surrounding membrane peeled, it is soft, creamy and rich when cooked.

Sheep's trotter

A sheep's foot. Mostly bone and cartilage, it requires prolonged cooking to soften. It makes gelatinous stock and is used in broth and brawn.

Marrow bone

Lengths of ox leg and shin bone, with a fatty core, the marrow, which becomes soft when cooked, and is then scooped out to eat.

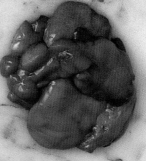

Sweetbreads

The pancreas (depicted) and thymus gland of a young animal. Initially soaked and blanched, they are pale, smooth and delicately flavoured.

Parma ham/Prosciutto di Parma

An Italian raw, air-dried ham, with DOC status. Made near Parma, Italy, from pigs nourished on the whey left over from making Parmesan cheese, it is dry-salted with sea salt for up to a month, then dried, without smoking, in the open air for at least eight months.

HAM AND BACON

Ham is the hind leg of a pig or hog, cured by salting then drying, and sometimes smoking. The many varieties of ham result from differing combinations of types of pig, curing recipes and methods of storage. Salting may be either 'dry', with salt, or 'wet', with brine, or a combination of the two, in varying concentrations, with added flavouring ingredients, and of varying durations. Once salted, ham is dried by hanging in currents of air, and/or smoking over differing woods, the differing durations of both influencing the ultimate ham. Some hams are cured for eating raw, typically thinly sliced, while others are intended to be cooked.

Bacon is the salt-cured side (flitch) of a pig. It may be dry-cured by rubbing it with salt and flavourings (the superior method), or wet-cured with brine, both immersed and usually injected into the meat. It may then be smoked. Unsmoked, it is known as 'green' bacon. Bacon must always be cooked. When cooked, wet-cured bacon often oozes a white watery foam and shrinks. Speck is the German word for, generally streaky, bacon.

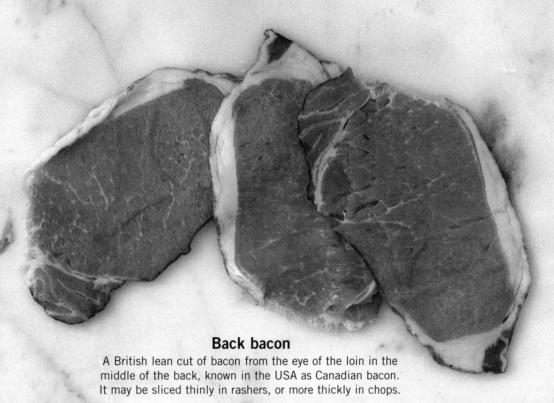

Back bacon
A British lean cut of bacon from the eye of the loin in the middle of the back, known in the USA as Canadian bacon. It may be sliced thinly in rashers, or more thickly in chops.

Streaky bacon
A cut of bacon from the belly, with alternating streaks of fat and lean meat, running parallel to the rind. Usually sliced thinly into rashers, in one piece it is called slab bacon.

Pancetta

An Italian style of salt-cured belly of pork, with regional variations, usually not smoked. Alternately streaked with fat and lean meat, it is an important ingredient in *soffritto*, the point of departure for many dishes of Italian and Spanish origin.

Lomo curado

A Spanish dry-cured, spiced eye of the pork loin in a casing. Extremely lean, it is typically eaten thinly sliced, dribbled with olive oil, as tapas.

Jamón

The generic Spanish word for ham. Two artisanal hams from Southwest Spain are especially of note: Jamón serrano, mountain ham, is produced in mountainous regions from white pigs; Jamón Ibérico is produced from the lean native black-hoofed Iberian pigs reared in the woodlands. Both are raw, air-dried, without smoking, and matured for a year or more. Eaten thinly sliced, they are fine flavoured though liable to be tough.

COOKED HAMS

Renowned ready-cooked and to be cooked hams include:

York ham   Named for a curing method used the world over. Dry salted and lightly or heavily smoked, then matured for several months, York ham is pale-pink, mildly flavoured, and considered best served cold.

Bradenham ham   An English ham made in Wiltshire, cured for six months in molasses with juniper berries and spices. Distinctive with its name branded on its black exterior, it has a delicate, sweet flavour.

Virginia ham   An American regional 'country-cured' ham, the most esteemed of which is Smithfield ham. Cured in the Virginia town of Smithfield, from nowadays grain-fed razor-back pigs, the ham is dry-salted with a mix that includes pepper, heavily smoked with apple and hickory wood, then aged for at least one year. Dark-coloured, lean and richly flavoured, it is often baked with a sweet glaze, and eaten hot and cold.

Kentucky ham   An American regional ham, made from Hampshire hogs fed on acorns, beans, clover and grains. dry-salted and smoked over apple and hickory wood and aged for a year. It has a delicate flavour.

Pragerschinken   From the Czech Republic, 'Prague ham' is brined for months, smoked over beech wood, then well-matured in cool cellars. It is considered best served hot.

Jambon de Paris   Also known as Jambon blanc and Jambon glacé, this lightly brined, unsmoked French ham has a very mild flavour and is eaten boiled and cold.

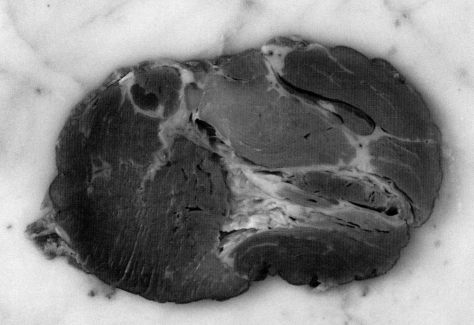

Westphalian ham
A German raw ham. Dry-salted, brined, scrubbed, then gently
smoked over beechwood and juniper twigs and berries, it is
dark with a distinctive, subtly smoky flavour.

Pork sausages

Fresh raw pork meat, in varying proportions of fat to lean, coarsely or finely ground, diversely seasoned, stuffed into a casing, traditionally an animal intestine; in the UK, rusk or meal is usually also added. Before eating, they must be cooked by grilling, frying or boiling.

Boerewors

Fresh 'farmer's sausage' from South Africa, made with coarsely ground pork and beef seasoned with coriander, nutmeg, cloves and vinegar, formed into a long coil and traditionally cooked on a braai (barbecue).

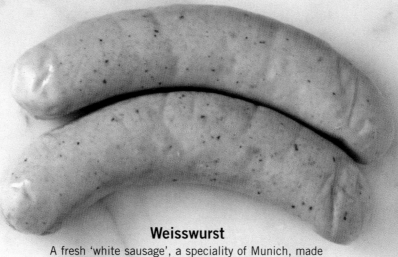

Weisswurst

A fresh 'white sausage', a speciality of Munich, made of ground veal seasoned with parsley. Having little flavour of its own, it is traditionally accompanied by a special sweet mustard.

Knackwurst

A plump German sausage of finely ground pork and beef, flavoured with cumin and garlic, air-dried then cool-smoked. It is served boiled or grilled, often with sauerkraut.

Bratwurst

A German pale fresh sausage of finely ground pork and veal, varying in size and seasoning according to its town of origin. It is usually grilled or fried.

Saucisson sec

A French large dried, unsmoked raw sausage, a Gallic version of salami. Made almost exclusively of pure pork and flecked with fat, it is matured from one to six months, developing a white powdery covering. It is eaten as is, sliced.

Chorizo

A Spanish sausage, essentially of chopped or minced pork spiced with paprika, and characteristically red. Varying regionally, it may be hot or mild, and smoked or unsmoked. When fresh and soft it is eaten cooked, often simmered in soups and stews.

Dried chorizo

Chorizo hung until dry and hard, the more common form of this Spanish sausage. Requiring no cooking, it is sliced and eaten cold. It is also an important cooking ingredient.

Salame di Napoli

A strongly flavoured, dried raw sausage from Naples. Made of coarsely ground pork and beef, studded with pork fat and seasoned with salt, garlic and chilli pepper, it is smoked while drying, and aged for two to four months. It is eaten cold, sliced.

⤵ **Haggis**

Minced sheep's pluck (heart, lungs, liver) mixed with oatmeal, onions, fat and seasonings, stuffed in a sheep's stomach and simmered. A Scottish speciality, it is traditionally served with bashed (mashed) neeps (swede) and tatties (potato).

⤵ **White pudding**

A sausage skin stuffed with oatmeal and suet, flavoured with onion. Called mealie pudding in Scotland, it is typically boiled, or sliced and fried.

Andouillette

A small fresh French tripe-based sausage. It differs from its larger relative andouille in that it is never smoked, and is generally grilled and served hot.

Black pudding/blood sausage

A sausage filled with blood (usually pig's), cereal and suet, flavoured with spices and herbs, then cooked. Typically served sliced and fried. Also called *boudin noir*.

Kabanos

A Polish hard sausage of coarsely minced pork, traditionally formed in long thin links and lightly smoked. It is eaten as is, or cooked.

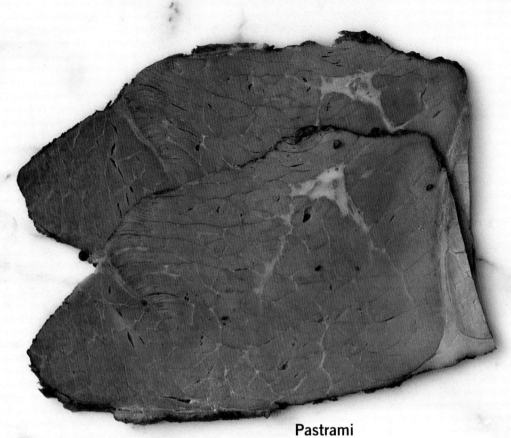

Pastrami

Trimmed beef brisket rubbed with a paste of salt, garlic, and spices including pepper, smoked then steamed. A speciality of New York Jewish cuisine, it is eaten hot or cold, typically thinly sliced on rye bread.

Corned silverside

The lean tough outer thigh beef muscle, with a layer of fat on one side, cured in a spiced brine, also called corned and salt beef. It is boiled and served hot, classically with carrots, and as a cold cut.

Chipped beef

Very thin slices of salted and smoked dried beef. Once an
American staple, it was commonly served in a cream sauce
on toast. It is often sold wadded in jars.

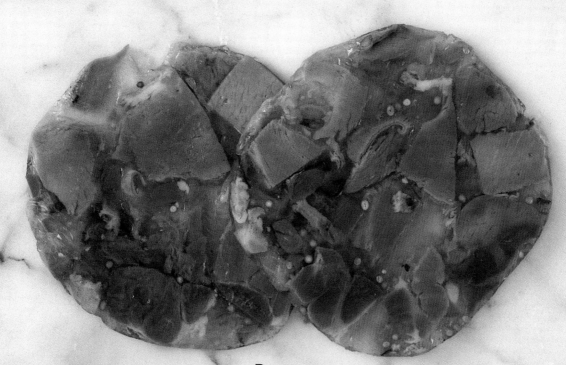

Brawn

A moulded preparation of the coarsely chopped boned meat of
a brined head, usually pig's, set in the jelly reduced from the
broth in which it was boiled. Called head cheese in the US, it
is served cold, sliced.

Poultry

Poultry is a generic term for domesticated barnyard fowl reared as food, both for meat and eggs; it includes chicken, duck, turkey, goose and guinea fowl. The meat is considered in this chapter; eggs are covered on p106–107.

Chicken is the most commonly consumed of all poultry. Once a luxury, modern intensive-rearing practices have made it a relatively inexpensive meat, albeit often lacking in flavour and texture. Whereas formerly a chicken's age and breed were the distinguishing factors in eating quality, nowadays the diet and the method of rearing, whether genuinely free-range or battery, also make a difference. Chicken is a particularly versatile meat, able to be prepared in a myriad ways: it may be baked, roasted, grilled, fried, poached, braised or stewed; its inherent lack of flavour making it a blank canvas for a diversity of flavourings.

Game denotes wild animals hunted for sport; over time, the distinction between domesticated animals and game has become less defined with the modern practice of rearing 'game' in protected circumstances, then releasing them, to ensure stock. Some 'game' is actually farmed. Game birds, or feathered game, include pheasant, partridge, quail, grouse, pigeon and wild duck. Many wild game birds are protected, with their hunting being permitted only during specified seasons. (British seasons are given in this chapter.)

The flesh of truly wild game is leaner, more compact in texture and more intensely flavoured, than its domesticated counterparts, the result of the greater exercise and natural diet involved in surviving in the wild. Handling in the field, hanging and, above all, the animal's age, determine the eating quality of a particular bird, and therefore how it is best prepared.

Despite the pre-emptive medication of intensively reared birds, in some countries many are infected with salmonella bacteria, a common cause of food poisoning. Because salmonella is destroyed by high heat, thorough cooking renders the meat safe to eat; pale fleshed fowl should never be eaten raw or underdone. Care must also be taken not to contaminate other foods when storing and handling raw poultry.

Poulet de Bresse

A top quality, blue-footed breed of chicken, raised in the Bresse region of France to strict regulations. It is identified by a leg ring

Chicken

A domesticated fowl raised, either free-range or, more commonly, intensively, for its meat. Classified by weight, age when slaughtered, diet, and/or method of rearing, it is generally lean with pale, tender, delicately flavoured breast meat and darker, slightly stronger-flavoured leg meat.

Cornish hen

A small hybrid chicken, having excellent meat. Bred mainly in the USA, they are slaughtered between four and six weeks old, weighing up to 1.2kg/2½ lbs. Also called a Rock Cornish game hen.

Poussin

A baby chicken, four to six weeks old, weighing 350–500g/12–18oz. Tender and delicate in flavour, they are usually grilled or roasted. In the USA, poussin are often called squab.

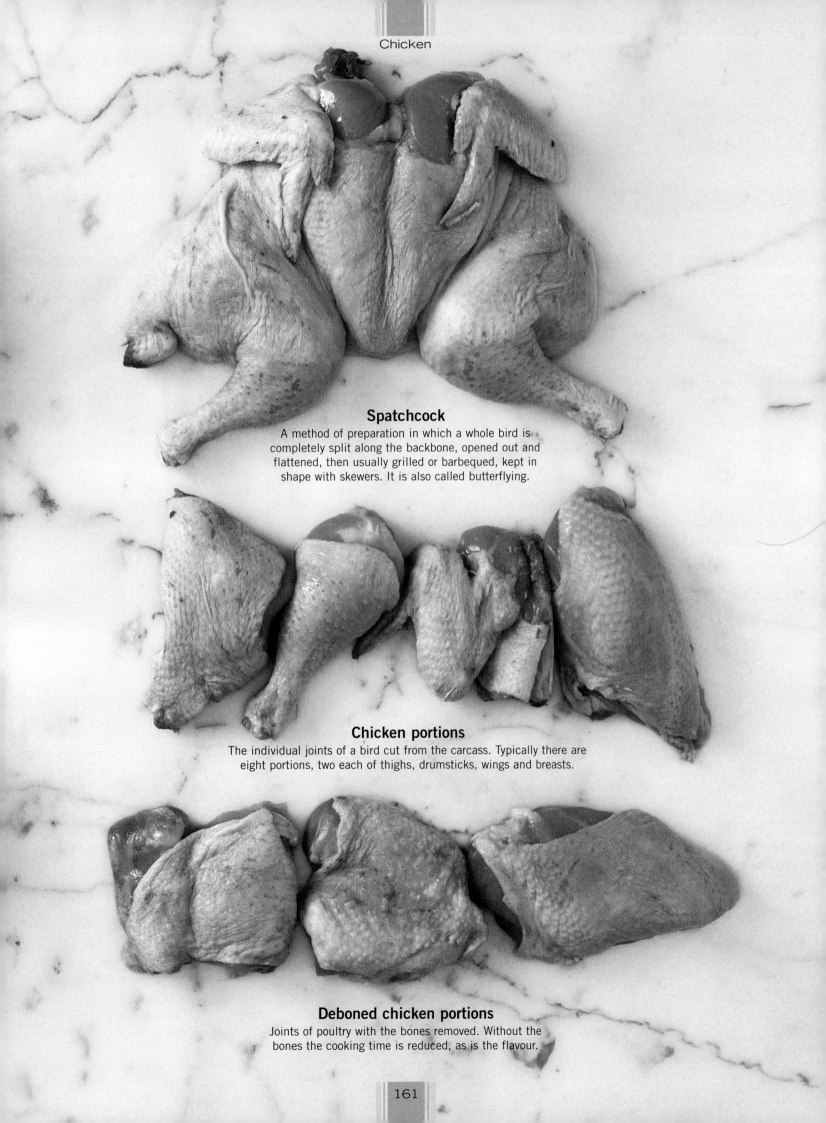

Spatchcock
A method of preparation in which a whole bird is completely split along the backbone, opened out and flattened, then usually grilled or barbequed, kept in shape with skewers. It is also called butterflying.

Chicken portions
The individual joints of a bird cut from the carcass. Typically there are eight portions, two each of thighs, drumsticks, wings and breasts.

Deboned chicken portions
Joints of poultry with the bones removed. Without the bones the cooking time is reduced, as is the flavour.

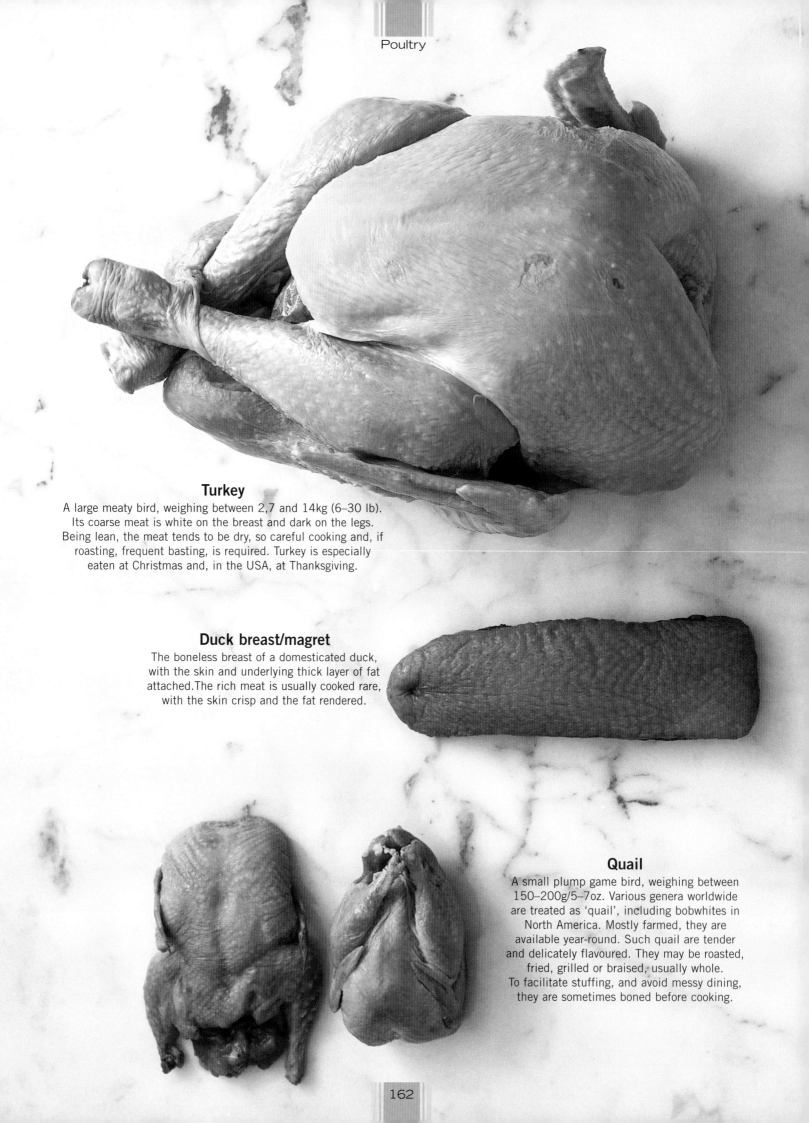

Turkey

A large meaty bird, weighing between 2,7 and 14kg (6–30 lb).
Its coarse meat is white on the breast and dark on the legs.
Being lean, the meat tends to be dry, so careful cooking and, if
roasting, frequent basting, is required. Turkey is especially
eaten at Christmas and, in the USA, at Thanksgiving.

Duck breast/magret

The boneless breast of a domesticated duck,
with the skin and underlying thick layer of fat
attached.The rich meat is usually cooked rare,
with the skin crisp and the fat rendered.

Quail

A small plump game bird, weighing between
150–200g/5–7oz. Various genera worldwide
are treated as 'quail', including bobwhites in
North America. Mostly farmed, they are
available year-round. Such quail are tender
and delicately flavoured. They may be roasted,
fried, grilled or braised, usually whole.
To facilitate stuffing, and avoid messy dining,
they are sometimes boned before cooking.

Goose

An adult female of a genera of large, web-footed birds. Domesticated, though not intensively reared, goose is at its best in autumn and winter, and was traditional European festive fare. With a large rib cage, it has less meat than its size would seem to indicate. It is renowned for its copious, extremely soft fat, in which it is classically cooked and preserved (confit).

Liquid duck fat

The rendered (melted and strained) fat of a duck.
With a melting point of 52°C (126°F), it is the medium for
cooking and preserving duck in confit, and makes superb
roast potatoes.

Duck liver pâté

A smooth rich paste made from ground duck's livers and various
seasonings. The fattened livers (foie gras) of force-fed ducks
make an especially rich version.

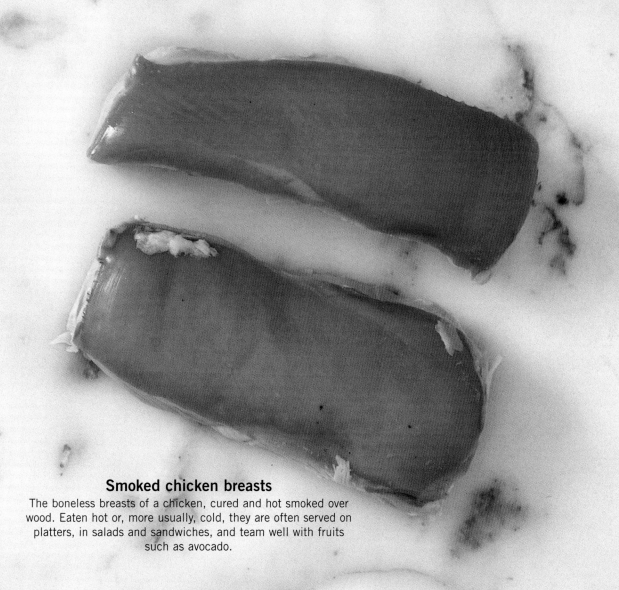

Smoked chicken breasts
The boneless breasts of a chicken, cured and hot smoked over wood. Eaten hot or, more usually, cold, they are often served on platters, in salads and sandwiches, and team well with fruits such as avocado.

GIBLETS
These are the edible internal organs (heart, liver, gizzard and neck) of a fowl. The liver excepted, they are mainly simmered in water for stock and gravy. The livers of all poultry and game birds should be trimmed of any green tinging, which will taste bitter. Generally cooked so the centres remain pink, the livers are served on toast, pasta and salads, or ground into pâté. In France, giblets are used in a stew (*alicot*), while preserved goose gizzards (*gésiers*) are served on salad leaves.

Foie gras, literally fat liver, is the liver of a duck or goose grossly enlarged by force-feeding the birds with maize. A prized delicacy, it is rich and silken-textured. It is sold raw, cooked fresh in cans, semi-cooked and pasteurized, and preserved in its own fat.

Wild duck

A non-domesticated water fowl. Of the many species, mallard, the largest, is the most common; it has a layer of fat beneath its skin and rich, though lean, dark meat.

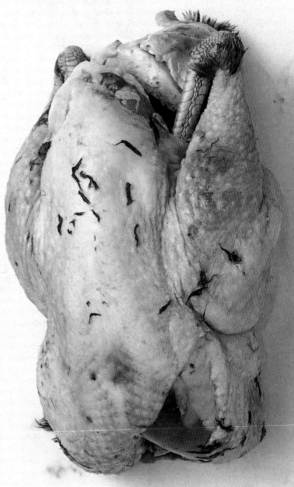

Pheasant

A medium-sized game bird, often reared in captivity then released for capture. It has a relatively mild gamey flavour, with the breast more delicate and tender than the darker, sinewy leg.
Often sold as a brace, comprising a hen and cock, the hen is considered better eating.

Grouse

A truly wild, small game bird found on the northern British moors. Its dark red flesh is rich and intensely gamey. One bird provides a single portion.

PREPARATION

Game birds are traditionally hung, unplucked, to tenderize them and develop their flavour, the length of time depending upon the bird, the weather, and taste. (Wild birds may contain remnants of shot that must be removed before eating.)

Having had to search for food, wild game is by nature lean. The consequent tendency to be dry when cooked can be avoided by barding and/or basting. Young, tender birds are simply roasted in a hot oven, the darker-fleshed birds rare or pink. Older, tougher birds are better braised. Traditional British accompaniments for roasted birds are bread sauce, fried breadcrumbs, croûtes, gravy, watercress and fruit jelly.

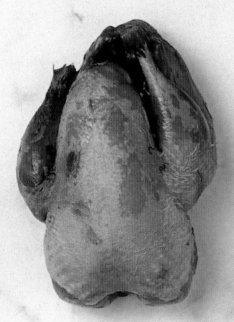

Partridge

A small European game bird, of two main species: the more esteemed grey or English partridge, with pale, fine, delicately flavoured flesh; and the nowadays more common larger, French or red-legged partridge.

Pigeon

The plump-breasted European wood-pigeon, at its prime in autumn, is considered the best to eat of the many wild species, having dark dense flesh with a gamey flavour. Squab, or young pigeon, are commercially reared, and are more tender than older wild birds.

IN SEASON

The shooting season for game birds varies around the world, depending on the species. Fresh birds are only available during the appropriate season, but frozen birds may be found at other times of the year.

The British seasons are:

Grouse: 12 August to 10 December.
Pheasant: 1 October to 1 February.
Partridge: 1 September to 1 February.
Wild duck: 1 Sept. to 31 January, or until 20 February below the high-tide mark.

Guinea fowl

A domesticated and wild bird, smaller and more meagrely fleshed than chicken. With a pheasant-like texture, the dark meat is slightly gamey and tends to be dry.

Fish & Seafood

In the broadest sense 'seafood' is any water-dwelling edible, the water being fresh or salty. It thus encompasses fish, shellfish and seaweeds. Fish are defined as cold-blooded aquatic vertebrates possessing fins and gills. Shellfish, aquatic invertebrates whose outer covering is a shell, comprise crustaceans, characterized by jointed limbs, segmented bodies and exoskeletons, and molluscs, variously gastropods (single shelled), bivalves (with double-hinged shells), or cephalopods (mostly with a modified internal shell). Seaweeds are plants: marine algae distinguished by their coloration.

Within these groups are a multitude of species. The names by which many are popularly known are confusing; different species are given the same name and this is compounded by there being a range of names for the same seafood. To identify a seafood, the principal alternative vernacular names, along with the Latin, are listed.

Names notwithstanding, fish can be divided into categories according to their size, shape, flesh density and fat content. For the cook, these characteristics are what matter; within a category one fish can be substituted for another.

Even with increasing aquaculture, much seafood consumed is wild. Therefore seafoods of the same species will not necessarily be uniform in flavour, as their habitat, and thus their diet, vary. For safety's sake, even more than flavour, it is important to be sure of their source.

Generally, fish is best eaten very fresh. Being cold-blooded, fish have enzymes effective at the temperature of their home waters; refrigerated, they continue to decompose. To slow this process, fish were dried, salted, pickled and smoked. Despite modern methods of preservation, many traditional methods are still practised for the flavour they impart.

Typically seafoods need little cooking – just until the muscle protein coagulates and becomes opaque; with fragile connective tissue, short muscle fibres and relatively low fat, they become dry and toughen or disintegrate if cooked beyond that point. Very fresh fish and shellfish may be eaten raw.

Bream (*Abramis brama*)
A freshwater fish of the carp family, also called bronze, common or carp bream. Favouring muddy bottoms, it needs scaling before cooking, and is bony.

Carp (*Cyprinus carpio*)
A large freshwater fish, the commonest of many carp species. With firm, though often coarse, flesh and easy bones, it is esteemed in C. Europe. Carp can acquire a muddy taste, countered by soaking in acidulated water. Its strong scales, gills and gall sac should be removed before cooking.

Salmon trout (*Salmo trutta*)
The sea-going form of various trout species: in the UK, called the migratory brown trout, or sea-trout; and in the USA, confusingly, often simply 'trout'. Their flesh is pink and oily. (See also Trout opposite.)

Catfish
A name given to many types of fish, both freshwater and marine. Typical characteristics include long, whisker-like barbels around the mouth, broad flat heads, and tough scaleless skin. The N. American Ictaluridae family of catfish has firm, mildly flavoured flesh with many small bones.

Salmon

A large migratory fish comprising six species: Atlantic salmon (*Salmo salar*); and five Pacific salmon of the Oncorhynchus family; the Chinook or king salmon (*O. tshawytscha*) being the most prized. To varying degrees, all have characteristically pink or reddish, compact oily flesh; farmed salmon is softer, fattier and usually less flavoursome than wild.

Bass

A freshwater fish, characterized by its sharp dorsal fin. Though various fish are so-called, true bass are members of the perch family. Their flesh is white, firm, and lean.

Tilapia

A small herbivorous freshwater fish, also called St Peter's fish. Much farmed, it is densely scaled, with white, sometimes tinged pink, lean, fine-textured flesh.

Trout

An extensively farmed freshwater fish of the salmon family. According to species it has pinkish or white, moderately oily, firm flesh, with a delicate, sometimes muddy, flavour. Called the steelhead trout in the USA. (See also Salmon trout opposite.)

Pike (*Esox lucius*)

A voraciously carnivorous freshwater fish. It has firm, lean, dryish flesh with many y-shaped bones. As large pike are tough, medium-size fish are preferred for cooking.

Red Mullet

A small fish of the Mediterranean and European Atlantic, also called goatfish in the USA. Distinctively crimson and heavily scaled, it is prized for its firm, flaky, flavoursome white flesh and its liver, a delicacy. It is best grilled or pan-fried.

John Dory (*Zeus faber*)

A thin-bodied, round fish found in deep water worldwide. With a large head and cavity, only one third of the whole fish is edible fillet, made up of white, bone-free, firm-textured, flavourful flesh. Also called St Peter's fish due to the distinguishing mark on the side, said to be the apostle's thumbprint.

Sea bass (*Dicentrarchus labrax, D. punctatus*)

A European silvery coloured marine fish, also called salmon bass. With soft, slightly flaky, moist, delicately flavoured white flesh, relatively free of bones, it is highly prized. It has quite oily skin and may be cooked by most methods.

Monkfish
(*Lophius piscatorius*)

A demersal (deep-water) marine fish which can attain huge size. Generally sold headless and skinned, the otherwise boneless 'tail' end has a single central cartilaginous spine, and white flesh so dense in texture that it is compared to lobster. The fine purplish membrane should be removed before cooking.

⇦ Grey mullet
(*Mugilidae* spp.)

A many specied inshore marine fish of warm and temperate waters worldwide. Silvery grey and covered with scales, their flesh is white and delicate but, being herbivorous bottom-feeders, it can be muddy.

Gurnard ⇨
(*Triglidae* spp.)

A demersal marine fish of warm and temperate waters. All species have a large bony head atop a cone-shaped body and firm, lean white flesh inclining to dryness. Called sea robin in the USA.

Mackerel

A medium-sized shoaling fish of the family Scombridae. Their firm flesh has a strong flavour; being high in oil, they spoil quickly, and are best cooked by dry methods. Mackerel are often served with a tart sauce, traditionally gooseberry.

Hake (*Merlucciius* spp.)

An oceanic fish of the cod family, growing up to one metre (39in) long. Lean and delicately flavoured, its white flesh has a soft milky texture, with the relatively few bones being easy to remove. It suits most methods of cooking.

Bonito (*Sarda* spp.)

A fish of the Scombridae family, which comprises many species of large pelagic (surface-feeding) fish, including tuna and mackerel. Bonito are found in the Atlantic and Mediterranean; a Pacific relative is known as skipjack. With compact, light-coloured, strongly flavoured flesh, it is prepared in the same manner as tuna: fresh it may be cooked as meat, often cut into steaks (the best coming from the belly). It may also be eaten raw, thinly sliced. Much tuna is canned (see p198) and, in Japan, bonito is dried, and shaved.

Trevally

A name used for various marine fish of the family Carangidae, common in tropical surface waters but also found in temperate waters, particularly of the Indo-Pacific and Australasia. Their white flesh is strongly flavoured, tending to be dry.

King mackerel (*Scomberomorus* spp.)

A large oceanic fish found in warm waters worldwide, one of the species of Spanish mackerel, also called kingfish. Highly esteemed for its compact, oily flesh and fine flavour, it is prepared as steaks, grilled and baked, smoked and, in SE Asia, curried.

Grouper

A medium to large marine fish of the genus *Epinephelus*, known as groper in Australasia, found in rocky warm and tropical waters worldwide. Often sold as steaks to be grilled or fried, its firm, flaky, fine-flavoured, white flesh is excellent eating.

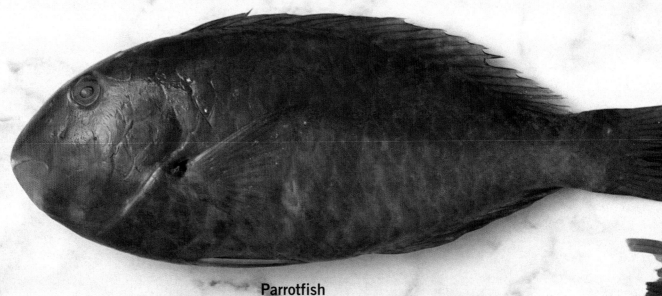

Parrotfish

A colourful small to medium-sized marine fish of the family Scaridae, with teeth fused together like a beak, found worldwide in reefs of warm and tropical waters. Often cooked whole, it has flaky white flesh with excellent eating qualities.

Barracuda

A long, narrow, marine game fish of genus *Sphyraena* found in the reefs of tropical waters worldwide. The great barracuda can cause cigatuera poisoning in humans who eat it. Smaller, non-toxic species have firm, white flesh tending to become dry when cooked.

Emperor

A medium-sized marine fish of the Lethrinidae family, mostly found in the reefs of tropical Indo-Pacific waters; also called capitaine. With moist, white flesh it has excellent eating qualities and suits most methods of cooking.

Red snapper

A medium-sized, red-skinned marine fish of several species of the family Lutjanidae, found in warm waters worldwide. Beneath its many scales its firm, lean, white flesh is good to eat and suits most cooking methods.
The fish known as snapper in Australasia belongs to the family Sparidae.

WHEN TO COOK?

Some non-bony fish tend to have an ammoniac smell, a natural result of their metabolism. To counteract the salinity of the sea and maintain an osmotic balance they make urea in their blood and tissues. After death the urea breaks up, producing ammonia, hence the smell.

While this tenderizes the flesh, eventually it becomes too strong. Therefore, the ideal time to cook such fish is about two days after their death, when the beneficial, but not yet unpleasant, changes have occurred. The smell can also be reduced by soaking the flesh in acidulated water.

Skate/ray

'Flattened' bottom-feeding marine fish of the Rajidae family. The wing-like pectoral fins are the part eaten, usually sold already cut off and skinned. Cartilaginous with no true bones, long strands of soft white flesh part easily from the skeleton when cooked. Classically, skate wings are poached and served with black butter.

Dogfish

A small shark, of many species, variously known as huss, flake, rock salmon, grayfish and rigg. All have tough, rough skin and a cartilaginous skeleton with no true bones. Their firm, moderately lean flesh is strongly flavoured so can withstand robust cooking; they are often deep-fried for fish and chips.

Shark

A marine fish, of many species, varying in size, all with cartilaginous skeletons and no true bones. The flesh is dense, meaty, and slightly oily with a good flavour; the pink flesh of porbeagle and mako sharks is likened to veal. Most methods of cooking are suitable, grilling especially; care must be taken not to overcook it.

Cod

A large round marine fish of the family Gadidae, found in cold Pacific and Atlantic waters. With lean, moist, chewy white flesh which separates into large flakes and large obvious bones, it is excellent to eat and suits most methods of fish cookery.
Scrod (USA) and codling (UK) are small cod.

Whiting
(*Merlangius merlangus*)

A small marine fish of the cod family, found from the Mediterranean to the N. Atlantic. Its bland, very lean, rather dry, fine-textured flesh readily falls apart on cooking.

Pollack
(*Pollachius pollachius*)

A marine fish of the cod family, found in the E. Atlantic.
Because its lean white flesh tends to be dry and is less
well-flavoured than cod, it is not esteemed as a food fish.
Another fish of the cod family, called pollock (*P. virens*) in
the USA, and saithe, coalfish or coley in UK, has coarse,
greyish flesh which whitens on cooking.

Haddock
(*Melanogrammus aeglefinus*)

A medium-sized demersal marine fish of the cod family,
found in the Atlantic. Softer, with smaller flakes than cod,
its lean, sweet-flavoured white flesh can be prepared and
cooked in the same way as cod.

Brill
(*Scophthalmus rhombus*)

A flat marine fish found in shallow European waters, closely related to the larger turbot. Oval in shape, with very fine scales and completely smooth skin, brill has lean white flesh, with good flavour and texture, which is considered inferior to that of turbot.

Lemon sole
(*Microstomus kitt*)

A flat marine fish of European waters, with smooth, slimy skin. Being sinistral (eyes on the left of the head), it is not a true sole, which are dextral (right-sided eyes). It has soft, well-flavoured, white flesh and is suited to cooking as sole, grilling especially.

Turbot
(*Psetta maxima*)

A large flat marine fish of inshore European waters. Its lozenge-shaped body has tough scaleless skin, the upper dark side covered with small bony tubercles. With firm, dense, moist, white flesh and an excellent sweet flavour, it is highly esteemed. Traditionally poached whole; because of its size, nowadays it is often cut into steaks. Small fish are called 'chicken turbot'.

Halibut
(*Hippoglossus* spp.)

The largest of the flat fish, found in the cold, deep waters of the northern Atlantic and Pacific. Its white flesh is close-textured and well-flavoured, though prone to dryness. Because of its size it is usually sold cut into steaks.

Plaice
(*Pleuronectes platessa*)

A flat fish of European waters. Orange or red spots dot its eyed brown skin; its blind side is pearly white. Its firm, white flesh can be delicately sweet if it lived on a sandy sea bed.

Eel

A long snake-like fish, mostly of the genus *Anguilla*, which spawns and dies at sea but spends most of its life in freshwater, where it is caught. Beneath the tough, difficult to remove, smooth scaleless skin, it has firm, oily pinky-white flesh, delicate yet rich. It is typically stewed, grilled or smoked.

Lobster (*Homarus* spp)

A marine crustacean of cold N. Atlantic waters,
with claws for the first of its five pairs of legs
and a smooth jointed abdominal shell.
The American species, *H. americanus* (the best
known of which is the Maine lobster), is deep
green when live. It is larger than its dark blue
European relation (*H. gammarus*). When cooked,
the shells of both become bright red.
The most esteemed of crustaceans, lobster has
dense-textured, rich and sweet flavoured white
meat in the tail (abdomen) and claws.
The creamy liver, called tomalley, found in the
thorax, and the coral or roe of hen lobsters, both
green, are delicacies, and are stirred into sauces;
the shell may be used for stock.

SLIPPER LOBSTERS

Marine crustaceans of the family Scyllaridae, found in warm or temperate waters worldwide, variously known as bay, flathead and shovel-nosed lobsters and, in Australia, as bugs. Though varying in size, and colour, all species are flattish in shape with shovel-shaped feelers at the front, and extremely hard shells. The edible white, sweet, succulent flesh is found in the tail.

A major species, *Thenus orientalis*, or Moreton Bay bug, reddish-brown with a dull yellowish tail, is found in muddy inshore coastal waters of N. Australia. The dull reddish Balmain Bug (*Ibacus peronii*) is found along the southern Australian coast.

Spiny lobster

A marine crustacean of the family Palinuridae, with ten legs but no claws, found in warm and temperate waters. Coloured reddish-brown or purple, or in some species greenish, when live, it has a spiny shell, which becomes bright red when cooked. Its flesh, in the tail and legs, is white, dense-textured and sweet. It is often sold as uncooked, frozen tails. Spiny lobster is also called rock lobster, crayfish in Australasia and South Africa (not to be confused with freshwater crawfish), and langouste in France.

Norway lobster (*Nephrops norvegicus*)
A marine crustacean, resembling a small lobster, also called
Dublin Bay Prawn, langoustine, scampi and Florida lobsterette.
Measuring up to 24cm (9in) in length, with a pink or orange-red shell,
its relatively little meat, mostly in the tail, is sweet and delicate.

SHRIMP VS PRAWN
The terms 'shrimp' and 'prawn' are used differently in the UK and USA. In the UK, 'shrimp' denotes Crangonidae and the smaller species, while 'prawn' is used for Palaemonidae and larger forms.

In North America, 'shrimp' is used to describe both species, no matter what their size. If the term 'prawn' is used at all, it signifies the smaller species.

Brown shrimp (*Crangon crangon*)
A mostly estuarine decapod crustacean, and the
most common European shrimp. A maximum of
6cm (2½in) long, it is a translucent grey or brown,
becoming brown when cooked. After brief boiling
in salt water, the meat is pulled from the tail for
eating, often potted in butter.
In the NE Pacific, *C. franciscorum* represents the
same genus, known there as California, bay, or
grey shrimp.

Common prawn
(*Palaemon serratus*)

A coastal marine decapod crustacean, the prevalent edible prawn. With a market length of 7–8cm (3in), it is almost colourless when alive, becoming orange-red when cooked. Called shrimp in the USA, they are usually sold there with the heads removed.

PRAWNS

There are thousands of species of prawn, of many sizes and hues, living in fresh and salt waters, both temperate and tropical. They have stalked eyes, antennae, 10 legs, and are encased in a jointed, multi-hinged carapace. Though not anatomically correct, the part of the prawn eaten, the meaty body, is often called the 'tail'. Raw, unshelled prawns are termed 'green'.

King prawn

A very large prawn, also known as jumbo shrimp in the USA. Categorized in the UK by size, as any prawn with a count of less than 123 per kg (head on/shell on), elsewhere the name is applied to specific species of prawn. The Australian Eastern King Prawn (*Penaeus plebejus*), a light reddish-brown with bright yellow appendages, is the best known.

(Atlantic) Blue crab
(*Callinectes sapidus*)

A decapod crustacean, principally found along the eastern seaboard of the
USA. Popular in its soft-shell state, when it has just shed its hard exo-skele-
ton, it is also called 'soft-shell crab'. Also eaten in its hard shell state, its
shell turns red once cooked. It is of excellent eating quality, yielding white
meat mostly from the claws but also the back fin, and brown meat.

Common brown crab
(*Cancer pagurus*)

A large European decapod crustacean known by various names. Its claws
contain white meat, and its body brown meat, both sweet with a delicate
flavour; the sweeter white meat is generally preferred.
Once cooked, by boiling or steaming, the small flakes of meat are picked
out of the shell. Its large liver is a delicacy. The gills, found immediately
behind the head, and also called 'dead-man's fingers', are not eaten.

Native oyster (*Ostrea edulis*)

A slow-growing bivalve marine mollusc indigenous to Europe, also called European, flat, or common oyster. It has rounded, flattish shells and greyish-white flesh. Its complex, slightly metallic, iodine taste is considered superior to other species, and is usually appreciated raw. Traditionally, wild oysters are only eaten in months containing the letter 'r', to avoid the summer months when spawning takes place.

Pacific oyster (*Crassostrea gigas, C. angulata*)

A fast-growing bivalve marine mollusc, cultivated worldwide, also called Asian or Japanese oyster and, in France, *huîtres creuses*. One of its frilled, elongated shells is concave. Best in the colder months, the greyish-white flesh has a fresh, briny flavour; when spawning in summer, it becomes soft and milky.

Blue/common mussel (*Mytilus edulis*)

A bivalve mollusc, found worldwide in most waters, and widely cultivated. Its thin, oblong, convex shell is dark blue or blackish. Its cream or orange flesh, edible raw, is usually cooked, typically in its scrubbed and de-bearded shells.

Abalone/paua/ormer

A large single-shell marine mollusc of the genus *Haliotis*, found on intertidal rocks. The part eaten is the large adductor muscle or 'foot'. Being tough, it is often beaten to tenderize it before cooking; unless cooked briefly it will toughen. Its flavour is delicate.

Scallop

A bivalve mollusc of the family Pectinidae, found on sandy seabeds worldwide. A prized delicacy, the parts eaten are the firm, sweet, succulent, plump disc of whitish adductor muscle, trimmed of its frill and black stomach and, in Europe but not N. America, the creamy, stronger-flavoured pointed orange coral or roe.

Whelks

Large marine snails, and thus gastropods, of the family Buccinidae. The part eaten is the muscular foot, which is tough and chewy. In the UK they are typically boiled in salty water then marinated in vinegar. Because they can absorb toxins from their prey, it is preferable to source them from professional gatherers.

Clams

A bivalve mollusc, of many different species worldwide, categorized variously as soft-shell (longneck) and hard-shell (littleneck or Quahog, the Native American name) clams. In North America, hard-shell clams are graded in ascending size as littleneck, cherrystone and chowder; carpet-shell clams, known in French as *palourde*, are a European hard-shell variety. Steamer, razor and geoduck clams are soft-shell varieties. Depending upon their size, clams can be eaten raw or cooked, steamed, baked and used in chowder.

Cockles

Generally small bivalve molluscs of many species, mainly of the families Cardiidae (true cockles) and Glossidae (heart-cockles). Because they live buried in sand, they need to be purged of grit before being eaten, raw or cooked, like clams or mussels.

PREPARING SQUID, OCTOPUS AND CUTTLEFISH

Squid Pull the tentacles, and with them the ink sac and entrails, away from the body. Cut the tentacles from the head in front of the eyes. Squeeze the head end of the tentacles and cut off the beak which pops out. Remove the transparent quill of cartilage from the body. Cut away the fins. Strip off the purple membrane. Rinse well.

Octopus and cuttlefish Cut the tentacles away from the head. Squeeze and cut away the beak as for squid. Cut head from body. Continue as below:

Octopus: Turn the body inside out. Remove the entrails and ink sac. Rinse well. Blanch in boiling water, cool, peel away the membrane, scrape off the suckers.

Cuttlefish: Slit the body and remove the bone, ink sac and entrails. Rinse and strip membrane.

With all, discard the entrails, beak, quill, bone and membrane. The ink sacs may be reserved to both flavour and colour a dish.

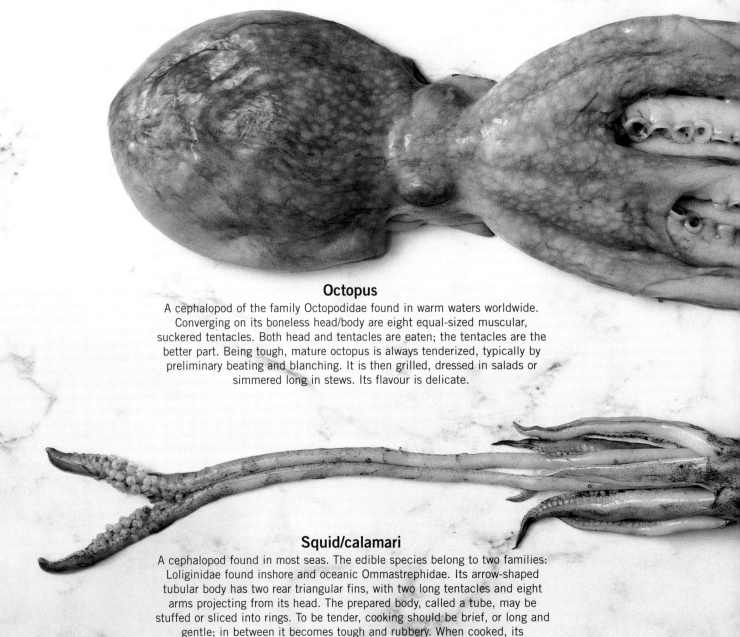

Octopus

A cephalopod of the family Octopodidae found in warm waters worldwide. Converging on its boneless head/body are eight equal-sized muscular, suckered tentacles. Both head and tentacles are eaten; the tentacles are the better part. Being tough, mature octopus is always tenderized, typically by preliminary beating and blanching. It is then grilled, dressed in salads or simmered long in stews. Its flavour is delicate.

Squid/calamari

A cephalopod found in most seas. The edible species belong to two families: Loliginidae found inshore and oceanic Ommastrephidae. Its arrow-shaped tubular body has two rear triangular fins, with two long tentacles and eight arms projecting from its head. The prepared body, called a tube, may be stuffed or sliced into rings. To be tender, cooking should be brief, or long and gentle; in between it becomes tough and rubbery. When cooked, its translucent flesh becomes opaque, and has a delicate sweet flavour.

Cuttlefish

A cephalopod of the families Sepiiadae and Sepiolidae. It has a flattish, oval body with a large internal bone, eight short arms and two tentacles protruding from its head. The body, arms and much of the head are eaten; the body is the better part. Large specimens may be tough, so will benefit from being tenderized, by beating or blanching, before cooking. Cuttlefish may be cooked in the same manner as squid or octopus but its meaty flesh is considered inferior.

Kipper

A cured herring: split open, cleaned, salted in brine, then cold-smoked over oak. A British classic, sold in pairs, they are cooked by frying, grilling or jugging.

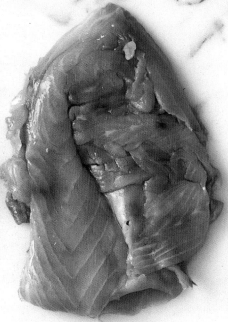

Cold-smoked salmon

Fresh salmon split into two filleted sides, brined or dry-salted, then hung over wood smoke for hours. Still raw, moist and smoky, it is eaten as is.

Smoked trout

Fresh trout prepared, salted, then hung over wood smoke. Usually hot-smoked, often whole but gutted, it may also be cold-smoked like salmon (depicted). With a mellow, smoky flavour, it is eaten as is or often made into mousse.

Smoked snoek (*Thyrsites atun*)

Snoek (not snook), an oily fish with long fine bones, butterflied and hot-smoked over oak. Popular in South Africa, it is eaten as is or made into pâté.

Peppered mackerel

Fillets of fresh mackerel, brined, topped with coarsely cracked black peppercorns, then hot-smoked over wood. Needing no further cooking, it is eaten cold as is, skinned and boned. It has a firm texture and a strong piquant flavour.

Salt cod/bacalao/bacalhau/morue

Cod opened flat, salted, then partially dried. Containing about 40 per cent water, it keeps well without refrigeration. After soaking in several changes of fresh water for up to 48 hours, it is variously cooked, usually initially poached, famously in the French *Brandade de morue*.

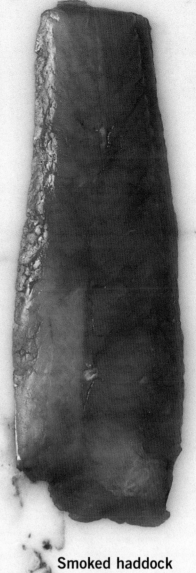

SMOKING FISH

Essentially there are two methods of smoking fish: cold-smoking and hot-smoking. With both, the fish is prepared in the same way. Whole, boned or filleted fish is salted, either dry-salted or immersed in brine, then hung to dry.

Cold-smoking: the smoke from wood shavings smouldering beneath the fish is kept at a low temperature, not exceeding 29°C (85°F) so that the smoke permeates the fish without cooking it.

Hot-smoking: after a period of cold-smoking, the temperature of the smoke is raised to about 85°C (180°F) and the fish is cooked.

The wood burned influences the flavour of the fish. Hardwoods are favoured; oak in the UK, hickory in the USA, manuka in New Zealand. Soft woods give a resinous bitter taste, but a good colour, so small proportions are sometimes added.

Commercially smoked fish is sometimes dyed prior to smoking to achieve a supposedly more appetising appearance; typically such fish is a vivid orange colour.

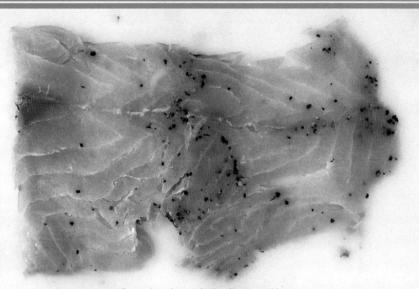

Gravlax/gravlaks/gravadlax
Boned salmon fillets cured with salt, sugar, pepper and chopped fresh dill. A Scandinavian specialty, it is usually eaten raw, thinly sliced, with dill mustard sauce.

Smoked haddock
Fresh haddock filleted, or beheaded, cleaned, split open, then brined and cold-smoked. It needs cooking and is classically poached in water or milk. Moist, smoky, with large flakes, it is a key component in kedgeree.
Whole smoked haddock, split but with the backbone left in, is known as 'finnan haddie' in Scotland and the USA.

Canned oysters
Shucked oysters in either brine, oil, or sauce, and sometimes smoked, preserved in a can. Having been heated in the process their texture is firm and dry; their flavour is fishy.

Canned mussels
Shucked mussels, in either brine, oil or sauce and sometimes smoked, preserved in a can. Having been heated in the process their texture is firm and dry; their flavour is fishy.

Taramasalata

A smooth paste of Greek origin, made from
salted fish roe (traditionally grey mullet, now
often smoked cod) blended with water-soaked
bread, olive oil, lemon juice and onion.

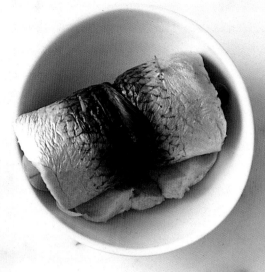

Rollmops

Butterflied, boned fillets of raw herring rolled
around a stuffing of onion and gherkin and
marinated in a spiced vinegar solution.

Caviar

The salted, ripe eggs (roe) of various species of sturgeon: dark grey
beluga are the biggest; golden to brown osciotr are medium-sized;
grey sevruga are small. For all, the best is lightly salted, or *malassol*.
It should be stored chilled, and never heated.

Canned tuna

Precooked tuna meat packed in oil, brine or
water and preserved in a can (tin). Graded by
size as fancy/ solid, chunks, or flakes, it is
either white meat (the better quality, from
albacore) or light meat (skipjack, yellowfin).

Canned anchovy

Small fish, filleted and salt-cured, then
canned in oil or packed in dry-salt.
Distinctively salty, they are used sparingly
to flavour food, especially in Mediterranean
cooking; soaking reduces their saltiness.

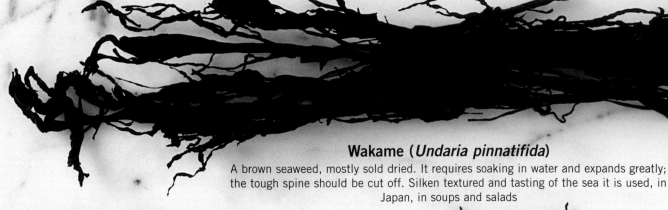

Wakame (*Undaria pinnatifida*)

A brown seaweed, mostly sold dried. It requires soaking in water and expands greatly; the tough spine should be cut off. Silken textured and tasting of the sea it is used, in Japan, in soups and salads

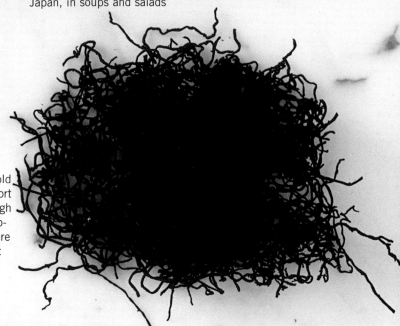

Hijiki (*Hizikia fusiforme*)

A brown seaweed, mostly sold dried in finely, shredded short pieces. As hijiki contains high levels of potentially carcino-genic inorganic arsenic, there are many cautions against eating it.

Konbu/kombu (*Laminaria spp*)

Kelp-related brown seaweeds. Naturally rich in monosodium glutamate, it is much used in Japanese cookery, where it is an essential ingredient in the soup stock, dashi. The dried, leathery strands are lightly wiped, not washed, to remove salt speckles before use.

Nori/laver/sloke/ (*Porphyra spp*)

A reddish seaweed dried to purple-black. In Japan, as well as wrapping sushi, thin sheets of nori are toasted and shredded as a garnish or crumbled over rice. In Wales, it is boiled to a thick purée and mixed with oatmeal to make laver bread.

Herbs, Spices & Seasonings

Flavourings are added to food to enhance its flavour. While their impact may be great, they are subsidiary to the food itself. They take the form both of things cooked with food, and those added to food once cooking is completed. In this chapter the concept of flavourings is broadly construed to include herbs, spices, salts, condiments, stocks, vinegars, oils and fats (except dairy fats which are discussed on p104).

A herb is defined as a plant whose green parts, usually the leaves, but sometimes the stalks, are used. For eons, herbs have been used for medicinal, cosmetic and culinary purposes; here only the last-named is considered. Herbs are used fresh and dried. When dried, the water is removed, leaving the essential oils which give the herb its flavour, effectively concentrating the flavour of the herb. Generally about one-third the amount of a dried herb equates to its being used fresh. However, fresh and dried herbs are not always interchangeable; most dried herbs lose their fresh 'top notes' and those with especially volatile oils lack their key flavour.

A spice is defined as any part of a plant other than the leaf, and may be the buds, bark, roots, rhizome, berries, seeds or stigma. Most spices are dried, many only acquiring their distinctive flavours by the enzymatic reactions triggered in the curing process. Their flavour is often heightened by dry-roasting.

A condiment is understood as a strongly flavoured savoury accompaniment to food, used at the table. Such flavourings are also used as seasonings in the kitchen.

Salty and sour flavours are derived from 'simple' salts and acidic fruit juices, and from complex fermented products, such as fish sauce, soy sauce and vinegar. These are often combined with spices and herbs to make mustards, pickles, chutneys, and sauces.

Stocks and fats, as well as being cooking media, impart flavour and, in the case of oils, are used to season.

Flavourings are not necessarily consistent, and should be used judiciously.

Basil

A warm-climate herb, with a clove-like fragrance. Its tender leaves are best fresh, added to dishes after cooking; heated, the essential oils dissipate. It has an affinity with tomatoes.

Dill

An umbelliferous herb, with aromatic, distinctively-flavoured, tender feathery green leaves. It is teamed with fish, potatoes, pickled cucumber, and sour cream. Cooked, its aroma dissipates. It is also called dillweed (USA).

Fennel

An umbelliferous herb, with large hollow stalks and feathery leaves: anise-flavoured sweet fennel has an affinity with fish and pork; wild fennel is bitter with no anise flavour.

Origanum/oregano

A wild marjoram, called *rigani* in Greece. Its coarser texture and thyme-like flavour, stronger than marjoram, suits robust flavoured dishes. Dried, it is more pungent.

Marjoram

Sweet marjoram has a thyme-like flavour but sweeter and more scented. More delicate than related oregano, it is added raw or when cooking is almost complete. It is stronger dried.

Parsley

A soft umbelliferous herb with a distinct yet unassertive, complementary crisp fresh taste. The flat-leaf variety, also called Italian parsley, predominant in Europe and the Middle East, is stronger than the curly-leaf variety.

Sage ✓

A herb whose velvety aromatic leaves have a pungent, camphorous flavour. Best used in moderation, its astringency counters rich, fatty foods. It withstands long cooking and dries well.

Rosemary ✓

The leathery, needle-like, aromatic leaves have a powerful peppery, camphorous flavour. Its astringency complements starchy foods and counters rich meats, especially lamb.

Thyme

A strongly aromatic herb with a pungent, warm, sharp flavour. Able to withstand long cooking, it has an affinity with tomatoes and marries well with other herbs.

Lemon thyme

A variety of thyme with a mild flavour overlaid with a lemony fragrance and tang. It is used as thyme, imparting a more subtle nuanced flavour.

Tarragon

French tarragon is a semi-hardy herb, aromatic with a delicate tart, anise-like flavour. Used in classic French cuisine, it has an affinity with chicken, eggs and cream sauces. Russian tarragon has little flavour.

Mint

Spearmint is the common 'garden' variety and the most-used culinary mint. Aromatic with a fresh, cool flavour, it has many applications: in yoghurt, with fruits and vegetables, or countering lamb's fattiness in sauces.

Peppermint has a characteristic scent and cooling menthol taste. It flavours confectionery, is used in baking, often as oil, and is drunk as an infusion.

Applemint, also called pineapple mint, is a variety whose variegated down-covered leaves have the scent and flavour of mint with a hint of green apples.

Bay

The leaves of the tree *Laurus nobilis*, also called sweet bay and bay laurel. Pungently aromatic when fresh, it is used whole, to flavour a wide range of cooked savoury dishes and milk puddings.

Balm/lemon balm

A herb with strongly lemon-scented foliage and a lemony mint flavour. It is used in fruit and green salads, soups, sauces, to season poultry and fish, and in various drinks.

Lovage

An umbelliferous herb with a very strong celery-like yeasty flavour. Although nowadays mostly used to flavour soups, in the past, the hollow stems were candied like angelica.

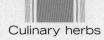

Coriander ✓

An umbelliferous herb with a distinctive aroma and flavour. The fresh tender leaves complement highly spiced dishes; the root is ground in curry pastes. It is also called cilantro and Chinese or Japanese parsley.

Vietnamese mint

A polygonum herb, not a mint, with a biting peppery hot taste. Used fresh in laksa, Vietnamese spring rolls and salads, it is also called laksa leaf, rau ram, hot mint, and Cambodian mint, as well as Vietnamese coriander.

Sorrel ✓

A spinach-like leaf with a sour, lemony taste. Midway between vegetable and herb, it is cooked in sauces and soups; young leaves are shredded raw in salads. Its sharpness offsets richness.

Salad burnet

A soft herb with a subtle, cool, cucumber-like aroma and flavour. Best raw, it is used in salads, chilled soups, sandwiches and fruit punches.

Garlic chives/ Chinese chives

Flat solid leaves with a mild garlic flavour, sometimes sold with the edible flower heads attached. They are popular in Asia, as a herb and a vegetable. Prolonged heat destroys their flavour.

Bouquet garni

A bundle of herbs, usually fresh but also dried, cooked in liquid dishes to impart flavour. The customary combination is thyme, parsley and bay leaf; other herbs or flavourings, like celery or leek, are sometimes added. They are tied together, wrapped in muslin, or packaged in 'tea bags' for removal at the end of cooking.

Herbes de Provence

A dried blend of the aromatic herbs traditionally used in Provençal France. Rosemary and thyme always feature; marjoram, basil, summer savory, lavender, bay leaf, sage and fennel seeds are often included.

Lemon grass/citronella
The lower leaf stem of a tropical Asian grass. Its fragrant lemony flavour, when crushed, is used in fish cookery and Thai curries. Being fibrous, if sliced, it should be finely, crosswise, and only the inner layers used.

Geranium
The highly fragrant, velvety leaves of a scented pelargonium; the many species include nutmeg (depicted), rose (the most popular), apple, lemon, and peppermint. Fresh, they perfume syrups, custards, cakes and jellies.

Lavender
The highly perfumed leaves and flowers of English lavender (*Lavandula angustifola*). Dried, they impart a floral flavour to custards, creams, vinegars, and conserves.

Angelica
An umbelliferous herb with a strong musky taste; the fleshy hollow stems are candied for use in cakes and, with the leaves, sweeten sour fruit dishes and flavour liqueurs.

Lemon verbena
The strongly lemon-scented leaves of an Aloysia shrub. Rich and sticky with lemon oil, (baked in desserts, or chopped into Asian dishes) they impart a fragrant lemony flavour, without lemon's acidity.

Violet

The fragrant, velvety, usually deep-purple, spring flowers of *Viola odorata*, also called sweet violet. Used to flavour and decorate, they are eaten raw in salads, infused in syrups and creams, and crystallized.

Borage

The star-shaped flowers of *Borago officinalis* (usually a vivid sky-blue, but sometimes pink). With a mild cucumber-like flavour, they are strewn over salads, floated in drinks and, sometimes, crystallized to decorate sweet dishes.

(Pot) Marigold

The bright yellow or orange daisy-like flower of *Calendula officinalis*. Pulled from the head, the petals, fresh or dried, tint food yellow by infusion and impart a slight peppery bitterness. The slightly peppery leaves can also be used, raw, in salads and sandwiches.

Rose

The flowers of the genus *Rosa*. The petals of scented blooms are conserved, crystallized for decorations, eaten fresh in sandwiches and, dried, perfume sweet dishes.

Nasturtium

The red, yellow or orange trumpet-shaped flowers of *Tropaeolum majus*. With a mild peppery flavour, they are decoratively scattered over salads, and stuffed. The leaves taste like cress.

Viola

The small purple and yellow flowers of *Viola tricolour*, also called heartsease, Johnny-jump-up and love-in-idleness and Cupid's flower. With no distinctive smell or flavour, they are used whole and fresh for their decorative qualities.

Elderflower

The creamy-white flower clusters of an elder tree, genus *Sambucus*. Raw, they contain small amounts of poisonous alkaloids and have a sickly aroma. Cooked, they safely impart a muscatel flavour to stewed fruits, notably gooseberries, and syrups.

Chives

The spherical mauve flowerheads of chives (see p59). Decorative, and with a delicate onion flavour, they are scattered raw over savoury salads.

Gillyflower/clove pink

The flowers of the carnation, *Dianthus caryophyllus*. Their sweet, clove-like fragrance historically flavoured syrups, conserves and vinegars, and they continue to decorate salads and flavour liqueurs and soups.

Allspice (whole)

The dried, cured, unripe berry of the tropical *Pimenta dioica* tree, also called Jamaican pepper and pimento. A pickling spice.

Allspice (ground)

Ground allspice berries. Used in cakes and fruit pies, its flavour resembles a compound of cloves, pepper, nutmeg and cinnamon.

Anise/aniseed

The seeds of *Pimpinella anisum*. The sweet liquorice taste flavours confectionery and baking and complements seafood dishes.

Asafoetida

A dried resinous gum with a fetid odour, becoming oniony when cooked. Small amounts flavour Indian pulses and curries.

Caraway

The seed-like halved, dried fruits of *Carum carvi*. Their pungent minty, nutty, anise taste flavours breads, cheeses, cabbage and meat.

(Green) Cardamom

Dried pods containing aromatic seeds with a warm, pungent eucalypt taste, which flavours curries, pastries and sweetmeats.

Cassia

The dried bark of tropical laurel trees. Resembling related cinnamon, it is more perfumed and pungent, with a bitter taste.

Cayenne pepper

The very pungent, finely-ground seeds of various fiery chillies. It is used, in small amounts, to add zest to cheesy dishes.

Celery seeds

The tiny, dried seeds of smallage, or wild celery. Their celery smell and bitter flavour is pronounced, so used sparingly.

Chilli flakes

Finely chopped dried chillies, with many seeds. Concentrated by drying, the pungency and flavour vary with the type of chilli.

Cinnamon (quills/sticks)

The thinly peeled bark of a tropical laurel tree, rolled into many-layered cylinders, dried. The flavour is infused into liquids.

Cinnamon (ground)

Very finely ground cinnamon bark. Delicate, sweet, woody, warm and fragrant, it is used in baking, fruit compotes and savoury stews.

Cloves ✓

Dried, unopened flower buds of a tropical myrtle tree. Aromatic, pungent, bitter and peppery, cloves should be used sparingly.

Coriander seeds ✓

The dried ripe fruits of *Coriandrum sativum*. Mild, aromatic and sweet, with hints of orange peel, it balances other spices.

Cumin seeds ✓

The fruits of *Cuminum cyminum*. Their distinctive, warm, earthy, aromatic flavour is used in Indian and Mid-Eastern cooking.

Curry leaves ✓

The leaves of the citrus tree *Murraya koenigii*. Their slightly spicy citrus aroma flavours curries, especially of S. India.

Curry powder ✓

A blend of ground spices, including coriander, cumin, mustard seeds, black pepper, chilli, fenugreek and turmeric.

Dill seeds ✓

The dried mature fruits of dill. Pungent, with a distinct anise, lingering character, they flavour pickles, fish, potatoes and breads.

Fennel seeds ✓

Aromatic, with a warm flavour like anise but less sweet, they season fish, Italian sausages, and Indian curries.

Fenugreek ✓

The faint celery-like smell, and sharp, bitter flavour, highlighted by roasting, often spices curries.

Galangal ✓

With a flavour like a mixture of ginger and pepper, this member of the ginger family is aromatic and pungent.

Ginger (ground) ✓

Powdered dried rhizomes of *Zingiber officinale*. With a warm, sweet aroma and lemony flavour, the pungency varies from delicate to hot.

Juniper berry ✓

The soft, ripe berries of a cyprus bush. Crushed, their aromatic pine/turpentine-like flavour is a foil for rich, gamey foods.

Liquorice/licorice root ✓

The roots and rhizomes of *Glycyrrhiza glabra*. Very sweet with an underlying bitterness and anise-like flavour, it is used in confectionery, and Asian stocks.

Mace

'Blades' of the dried aril that surrounds a nutmeg seed. Similar in flavour to nutmeg but more delicate, it spices seafood and meat dishes.

Mustard seeds

The dried seeds of three brassica plants. Fried whole, they taste nutty. Crushed, contact with liquids activates a volatile hot pungency.

Nutmeg (whole)

The dried kernel of the seed of the tropical nutmeg tree. As its flavour and aroma rapidly disappear, it is best freshly grated.

Nutmeg (ground)

Finely grated nutmeg seed. Aromatic with a robust warm, sweetish taste, it spices cakes, milk dishes and some vegetables.

Paprika

The red powder of ground, cured, dried capsicums. Ranging from sweet to mild to hot, it imparts a warm flavour and colour.

Black peppercorns

The whole unripe fruit of the vine *Piper nigrum*, fermented then dried until the skin oxidizes to black.

Black pepper (ground)

Milled black peppercorns. When freshly ground, their warm aroma, robust pungent flavour and lingering heat enlivens food.

White pepper (ground)

Milled, skinned, dried, partially ripe peppercorns. It is less aromatic but hotter in taste than black pepper.

Green peppercorns

Unripe fruit of *P. Nigrum*, brined or blanched, then dried. Their fresh hot bite is less pungent than other peppercorns.

Pink peppercorns

A pseudo-pepper, the ripe berries of *Schinus* trees, pickled or dried. The crushed seed has an astringent pine-like flavour with little heat.

Pickling spice

A mix of whole spices used for pickling. Traditionally it includes allspice, mustard and coriander seeds, black peppercorns, cloves, mace and often chillies.

Saffron

The dried stigmas of *Crocus sativus*. The dark-red threads have a penetrating aroma, a pungent, earthy, bittersweet taste and dye food golden.

Nigella
Seeds of love-in-a-mist (not black cumin or onion seeds). Nutty, peppery, acrid in taste, they spice vegetables, pulses, and breads such as naan.

Sichuan/Szechwan pepper
Split dried berries of the prickly ash tree. Fragrant, sharp, tangy and mouth-numbing, they are a foil to rich fatty meats. Also called Chinese pepper.

Sesame seed
The cream to black seeds of the sesame plant. With no aroma they are mildly nutty, sweet and moderately crunchy. (See also p94.)

Star anise
Dried, star-shaped fruits of an Oriental magnolia tree. Pungent, sweet, spicy, liquorice-like. Used in Chinese cookery.

Sumac
A coarse, moist powder of sumac berries. Its fruity astringency is used as a sour flavouring in Mid-Eastern cooking.

Tamarind concentrate
A paste extracted from ripe tamarind pods. Intensely acidic, it is used as a souring agent in tropical countries.

Turmeric
Rhizomes of the ginger family, boiled, dried and powdered. Used to colour food yellow, it has a sharp, bitter, musky flavour.

USING SPICES

Spices derive their characteristic aroma, and therefore flavour, from their volatile or essential oils, which are released by grinding or crushing the spice.

Over time the oils evaporate and a spice's aroma and flavour dissipate. Exposure to air hastens evaporation and oxidation, thus whole spices retain their flavour and aroma for longer than powdered or ground forms. Most spices should be ground as required.

To minimize deterioration, spices are best stored in airtight containers, cool, dry and away from direct light. It is advisable not to buy too large a quantity at a time.

Grinding spices oneself avoids the possibility that ready-ground spices, especially expensive ones, may be adulterated.

Vanilla pod/bean
The cured pod of a tropical orchid, with a black sticky mass of speck-sized seeds within. Pervasively fragrant, it has a sweet, rich mellow flavour.

Wasabi
The powdered roots of *Eutrema wasabi*, (Japanese horseradish). Mixed with water, it has horseradish-like pungency.

Za'atar/zahtar
A Mid-Eastern blend of thyme, sumac, salt and, usually, toasted sesame seeds, used as a seasoning.

Dukka(h)

An Egyptian specialty of a blend of coarsely ground, roasted nuts and spices. While the combination and proportions vary with the individual maker, it typically includes hazelnuts or chickpeas, sesame, coriander and cumin seeds, black pepper-corns and salt. Usually it is eaten on bread dipped into olive oil. It also serves as a crust for meat and a sprinkling topping.

Five Spice

A Chinese blend of five spices ground together: star anise, Sichuan pepper, cassia or cinnamon, cloves and fennel seeds. To these basic spices ginger, liquorice root, or cardamom are sometimes added. Star anise dominates. Fragrant with a sweet tangy aniseed character, it is used, sparingly, to season roast meats and poultry, and flavour marinades, and complements fatty meats like pork and duck.

Garam masala

The principal spice blend of North Indian cookery. While there are many versions, a basic blend includes cloves, cinnamon, green or black cardamom, black peppercorns and, often, bay leaf, mace, cumin and coriander; the spices are usually dry-roasted. It is added, whole or ground, initially or at the end of cooking. Warm and aromatic, it is used, mostly with meat or, to a lesser extent, with poultry or rice.

Chermoula

A Moroccan paste of spices and fresh herbs. In varying combinations and proportions the basic ingredients of paprika, garlic, cumin, fresh coriander (cilantro) or parsley, are blended with oil, lemon juice or vinegar and sometimes cayenne pepper, turmeric and chillies. Hot and spicy, it is mostly used as a marinade for fish.

Rock salt
Salt (sodium chloride) mined from underground deposits. The hard, crystalline lumps (clear, white or pink), must be ground to use. The flavour and colour derives from any impurities, which differ with the source.

Table salt
Fine grained salt with most of the impurities removed, and thus a simple salt taste, mostly used in cooking and as a table condiment. It usually contains an anti-caking agent, and sometimes iodine is added.

Sea salt
Salt (sodium chloride) obtained by evaporating sea water, either by the sun or artificial means. Formed as flakes or crystals, it varies in colour and flavour with natural minerals and impurities.

Salt flakes
Flat flakes of dried sea salt crystals raked from the bottom of evaporating pans. Soft and fragile, they crumble between the fingers and, due to their large surface area, cling to food.

Seaweed flavoured salt
Sea salt crystals mixed with ground, dried seaweed. Containing minerals, including iodine, seaweed enriches salt's nutritional profile and imparts more of a taste of the sea.

Fleur de Sel
The fine pure-white crystals scraped from the top of mounds of naturally evaporated sea salt, and so untainted by substrate from the bottom of the pond. It is highly prized.

Lemon pepper
A pungent, fragrant blend of cracked black peppercorns mashed with lemon peel/zest to release the citrus oil, dried then pulverized.

Celery salt
A finely ground mixture of salt and celery seeds pounded together. With a salty, celery flavour, it is used as a seasoning and condiment, complementing egg, vegetable and meat dishes.

SALT SCIENCE
Salt raises the temperature at which water boils. When the cooking water of vegetables is salted, it is less able to dissolve the natural mineral salts of the vegetables.

Dry salt extracts water from meat and vegetables by osmosis: so meat salted long in advance of cooking loses its juices; sprinkling with salt 'degorges' certain vegetables of bitter juices; and salting prior to pickling removes excess water, which would otherwise dilute the vinegar.

Extra virgin olive oil

Virgin olive oil with a fault-free aroma and flavour and a free acidity not exceeding 0.8g per 100g. The top grade of olive oil, it is used both as a cooking medium and as a flavouring ingredient.

Virgin olive oil

The natural juice of the fruit of the olive tree with the water removed, obtained solely by physical means under conditions, particularly thermal, that do not cause alterations in the oil. Olive oil classified as 'virgin' or 'fine' has a fault-free aroma and flavour and a free acidity not exceeding two per cent.

Olive oil

A blend of refined olive oil and virgin olive oil, sometimes called 'pure olive oil'. It has a free acidity not exceeding one per cent and is best used for cooking.

Canola/rapeseed oil

The oil extracted from the seeds of a subspecies of the rape plant, developed for its low erucic acid content. Predominantly monounsaturated, bland and odourless, it is suitable for cooking and as a salad oil. Canola oil is also called colza oil.

Sunflower oil

The oil extracted from the seeds of the sunflower plant, *Helianthus annus*. High in polyunsaturated fats and pale golden with a neutral flavour, it is used for cooking and as a salad oil.

Vegetable oil

Any oil, or a blend of oils, extracted from the seeds or fruits of plants. Its properties, flavour and colour vary depending upon its source; typically it is refined and bland. Generally, it is suitable for cooking or as salad oil.

Peanut/groundnut oil

The oil pressed from peanut (groundnut) kernels. Predominantly monounsaturated, if crude it is gummy with a distinct peanut taste; if refined it is bland. It is used as a salad oil and, with a high smoke point, is excellent for frying.

Sesame oil

The oil pressed from the seeds of the sesame plant: cold-pressed raw seeds yield pale oil with nutty nuances; toasted seeds yield dark amber fragrant oil with a strong nutty flavour, also called gingelly oil, which is added at the end of Asian cooking as a flavour accent. With a high smoke point, it is used as a cooking medium.

Grapeseed oil

The oil derived from the seeds of grapes. A by-product of wine-making, the seeds are cooked, milled, pressed or solvent extracted then, generally, refined. Bland, with a relatively high smoke point, it is good for sautéeing, and can be used as a salad oil.

Canola olive oil

A blend of olive oil and, predominantly, canola oil, in varying percentages. With the bland, but cheaper, canola oil subtly flavoured by the olive oil, it is an economical means of achieving a hint of olive oil in the cooking medium.

OIL TERMS

Olive oil grades: The International Olive Oil Council designates three grades of oil fit for human consumption as they are: extra virgin, virgin/fine, and ordinary/semi-fine virgin.

First pressed: The oil yielded the first time the fruit, nuts or seeds are pressed, with little or no heat, nor chemicals applied. Left in the state it emerges, unless filtered, the oil retains its natural flavours. Traditional, less-efficient oil presses do not extract all the oil in the first pressing and the paste is subsequently mixed with water, heated, and pressed again, yielding a poorer quality oil. Further oil may then be extracted with solvents.

Cold pressed: Oil extracted without any heat above 28°C (82°F). As heat has an adverse effect on oil, altering its flavour and hastening its decomposition, oil not subjected to heat retains its natural healthy attributes and flavours.

Pecan oil

The oil pressed from the kernels of pecan nuts. With the aroma and taste of pecans, more so if the nuts are roasted prior to extraction, it is used as a seasoning in baked goods, and in dressings.

Avocado oil

The oil extracted from the flesh of avocado fruit. Coloured green, it has a delicate buttery taste. It is used in the same way as olive oil and, with a high smoke point, is excellent for cooking.

Hazelnut oil

The oil pressed from the kernels of hazelnuts. Generally produced from roasted nuts, it is dark brown with the distinctive fragrance and strong, full flavour of hazelnuts. It is used in dressings and baked goods.

Macadamia oil

The oil pressed from the kernels of macadamia nuts. Pale gold with a delicate nutty, buttery flavour, it is used in dressings and baked goods and, having a high smoke point, is suitable for frying.

Argan oil

The oil extracted from the toasted seeds of the fruit of argan trees, found only in southern Morocco. A red-tinged gold oil, fragrant with a rich, nutty, fruity flavour, it is used for cooking, flavouring and finishing.

Mustard seed oil

The oil expressed from the seeds of various mustard plants. Its nutty, slight mustard flavour is only pungent if the seed meal is included, as in Indian versions. An effective preservative, it is used in pickles, and for cooking. (Only oil of seeds developed for a low erucic acid content should be consumed.)

Pumpkin seed oil

The oil pressed from pumpkin seeds. A dark russet-shot green, it has a nutty aroma and taste of pumpkin seeds, enhanced if the seeds are initially toasted. It is used for dressings and finishing; with a low smoke point, it is not cooked.

Soybean oil

The oil extracted from the seeds of soybeans (soya beans). Refined, it is pale yellow with a bland taste. With a high smoke point, it is used for cooking, and as a salad oil.

Walnut oil

The oil pressed from the kernels of ripe walnuts. With a distinctive walnutty aroma and flavour, enhanced if the kernels are initially toasted, it is a traditional cooking oil, now used mainly to dress salads.

Chilli oil

A bland vegetable oil or, sometimes, olive oil, in which hot red chillies have been steeped. Spicy and intensely hot, it is used, sparingly, as a flavour highlight and condiment, not as a cooking oil.

Apricot kernel oil

The oil pressed from the dried kernels of apricot pits. Golden, with a mild nutty flavour, it is used as a salad oil, in baked goods and, having a high smoke point, as a cooking medium.

Garlic and herb oil

Vegetable or olive oil in which garlic and fresh herbs have been steeped. Used to impart the particular flavours infused, it is cooked according to the characteristics of the base oil, and can also be used as a finishing condiment.

Lemon oil

The essential oil pressed from the yellow rind/zest of lemons. With a strong lemon fragrance and taste it is used, sparingly, as a flavouring. It is sometimes mixed with a vegetable oil as a condiment.

Hemp oil

The oil pressed from the seeds of *Cannabis sativa*. Non-narcotic, with a creamy nutty taste, it is eaten, as a flavour enhancer, primarily for the health benefits of its predominantly polyunsaturated fatty acids.

STORING AND USING OILS

Oils, like all fats, deteriorate with time. Exposed to air they oxidize and become rancid. This process is accelerated by light, heat and metal ions. They should therefore be used freshly extracted, and be stored in airtight, light-excluding, non-reactive containers away from heat. Unfiltered oil, with more vegetal matter suspended in it, oxidizes faster than filtered oil. Oil stored at low temperatures may solidify. On return to a warmer temperature, it will re-liquefy.

The smoke point of a fat is the temperature at which it breaks down and gives off smoke. It is typically lower in vegetable oils than animal fats. Pure fats smoke at higher temperatures than fats which contain other materials.

Sunflower margarine (tub)

Sunflower margarine (block)

Margarine

Margarine, formerly called oleomargarine or just oleo in the USA, is a butter substitute, nowadays made from various vegetable oils. In a complex series of processes, oil is purified, hydrogenated, fortified with vitamins A and D, coloured, and emulsified with a water phase, often including skim milk, sometimes flavoured with diacetyl and salt, and preservative added.

Like butter, it is 80 per cent fat, 20 per cent water and solids. The solidity of individual margarines is determined by the proportion of saturation of their constituent fats; hard block or stick margarine has more hydrogenated (artificially saturated and hardened), and less liquid oil than softer tub margarine.

Hard margarine can be used for cooking in the same way as butter. Soft margarine is essentially a spread and is not suitable as a cooking medium or for general baking.

Canola margarine

Olive oil margarine

Soya spread
A soft margarine made principally from soya/soybean oil. Containing a high proportion of liquid oil, it remains easily spreadable when cold. It is used as a spreading alternative to butter, but is not suitable for cooking or baking.

Suet
The hard, white fat which surrounds the kidneys and loin in beef and mutton. Finely chopped, it is used in certain English steamed puddings and pastries, stuffings and mincemeats. With a smoke point of 180°C/350°F it may be rendered for frying.

Lard
Pork fat rendered and clarified. Leaf lard, from around the kidneys and loin, is the best. Bland and white, it is used as a preservative, a spread and as a shortener in pastry. With its relatively high smoke point of 205°C/400°C, it is also used as a cooking medium.

Schmaltz
Chicken or, less usually, goose fat, rendered and strained. Often flavoured with onion, it is used in Jewish cuisine as a cooking medium and a spread, in a similar manner to butter.

Stock/bouillon cubes and powder

Stock cubes are highly concentrated solid extracts of stock compressed into moist cubes and sealed.
Stock powder and granules are made from dehydrated stock. Cubes, powder and granules are reconstituted
by dissolving in boiling water. They are chicken, beef, fish, vegetable and mushroom flavoured. All typically
contain a high proportion of salt and, sometimes, flavour enhancers, including monosodium glutamate.
Their flavour is usually less authentic than liquid stocks.

FRESH STOCK

Fresh stock, also called bouillon, is a strained liquid flavoured by the simmering of meat, poultry, game or fish and/or aromatic vegetables and other seasonings in water. Bones as well as flesh are used.

A white stock is made by putting ingredients directly into the liquid; in a brown stock, the ingredients are initially browned in fat or roasted, and their sugars thus caramelized. To extract maximum essence, the simmering is protracted, except in the case of fish, which becomes bitter after about 30 minutes. Skimmed of fat, well-made stock is clear. When boiled down, it becomes thick and jellied, and is known as glaze or glace.

Though any stocks may be made as brown stocks, generally white stocks are made with white poultry, fish and vegetables, while brown stocks are made with red meats. Typically, the vegetables used are carrots, onions and/or leeks, and celery, and the seasonings are parsley, thyme, bay leaf and whole black peppercorns. Shellfish stock derives its particular flavour and colour from the shells of crustaceans and molluscs.

Fresh stock is used as a basis for soups and sauces, so is not usually salted. However, commercially made stock and its derivatives vary greatly and may contain salt.

White stocks are more delicate in flavour than brown stocks. White chicken stock is the most universal of stocks. Of the brown stocks, beef is the most widely used. Veal bones produce a particularly fine stock which will set to a jelly and is highly esteemed. Fish, game, lamb, pork and ham stocks all have specific flavours so are generally only used in dishes containing the same key flavouring.

Fumet is a French term meaning a concentrated stock, and is especially used for fish stock, but also for mushroom stock. It is used to add flavour to a sauce.

Court-bouillon is a light stock made from stock vegetables and seasonings such as a bouquet garni and black peppercorns, usually acidulated with lemon juice, white wine or vinegar. It is used mainly for poaching seafood, especially fish.

Aspic is a clear savoury jelly of stock which is clarified then set, sometimes with the aid of gelatin(e), depending upon whether the stock was set when cold. It is used to embed, glaze and garnish cold meat, fish, poultry and egg dishes.

Dashi-no-moto

Instant dashi is Japanese soup stock made from flakes of dried bonito (tuna) and *konbu* (kelp), simmered together in water, and then dehydrated and powdered.

Fish sauce

The pungent, salty liquor drawn off fermented salted fish, and used as a flavouring and condiment. It is called *nam pla* in Thailand and *nuoc nam* in Vietnam.

Vegemite

A black paste 'extracted' from brewer's yeasts with vegetable seasonings. Strongly flavoured and salty, it is commonly eaten, spread thinly, on bread.

Marmite

A black entirely meatless paste 'extracted' from brewer's yeast. Strongly flavoured and salty, it is commonly eaten, spread thinly, on bread.

Bovril

Originally a concentrated beef extract, now a beefless savoury yeast extract, used as a stock or flavouring or, stirred into hot water, as a drink.

MISO

Miso is a rich savoury paste of fermented soya beans. Cooked soya beans are mixed with a starter culture (*koji*), (usually of rice, but also barley, or rye), salt and water and left to ripen from six months to three years. The fermented beans remain intact and are ground before use.

Miso ranges in colour from white (actually yellowish) to deep amber. It varies in thickness and saltiness: the lighter versions are milder and more quickly fermented; the darker versions more mature and stronger. All dissolve readily in hot water or stock.

Miso is much used in Japan, in soups and as a simmering liquid, to dress salads, and to flavour sauces and pickles.

Malt vinegar

Vinegar made from unhopped beer, derived from malted barley. Its brown colour is usually darkened with caramel. With a harsh, malty taste, it is primarily used in pickling. It is also the traditional vinegar to accompany fried fish and chips.

White vinegar

Malt vinegar either decoloured by filtering or distilled to make a very strong 'spirit vinegar'. Clear, colourless and harsh-tasting, it is used in pickling for aesthetic reasons.

Balsamic vinegar

Produced in Emilia Romagna, Italy, traditional balsamic vinegar is grape must, simmered to a concentrate and allowed to ferment and acetify. Then, for at least 12 years, it is progressively siphoned through a battery of barrels of decreasing size, each made from a different wood. Dark brown and viscous, with an aroma of wood and grapes, and richly sweet and sour, it is used sparingly as a condiment.

Industrial balsamic vinegar ranges from a 'semi-balsamic' to wine vinegar coloured and flavoured with caramel.

On a label, traditional balsamic vinegar is distinguished by the terms '*tradizionale*' and/or 'D.O.C' and the producer's and Conzorzie insignia. The bottle will be sealed with a wax or lead capsule.

VINEGARS

Raspberry vinegar

Vinegar, usually of white wine or cider, infused with fresh raspberries, strained, and typically sweetened with sugar. Traditionally diluted for a refreshing drink, it is also used as other flavoured vinegars.

VINEGAR

Vinegar is a sour liquid which results when an alcoholic liquid is exposed to air: aerobic bacteria oxidize the alcohol to acetic acid. The process is usually controlled by the addition of a starter, which includes a scum of desirable bacteria called the vinegar mother.

The flavours of vinegars vary according to the nature and quality of the base liquid, and the method of acetification. Normally vinegar contains from 4–6 per cent acetic acid, but its strength can be increased by distillation.

Tarragon vinegar

Vinegar, typically of wine or cider, infused with fresh tarragon. One of the most popular herb vinegars, it is classically used in Béarnaise sauce.

(Apple) cider vinegar

Vinegar made from fermented apple cider. Milder than wine vinegar, with a fruity taste of apple juice, it is consumed for its purported health-giving properties and used to deglaze, in court-bouillons, and in salad dressings.

Red wine vinegar

Vinegar made from red wine. The best is made by the slow, cool Orléans process. With a pronounced taste, the nuances depending on the base wine, it is used particularly in vinaigrettes, and to marinate and deglaze robust meat dishes.

White wine vinegar

Vinegar made from white wine. The best is made by the slow, cool Orléans process. It is used in sauces such as mayonnaise, beurre blanc and hollandaise, in court-bouillons, to deglaze, marinate and for aromatized vinegars.

VINEGARS

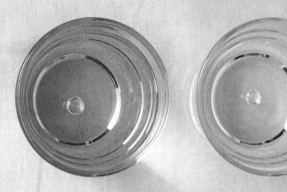

Japanese rice vinegar

Vinegar made from fermented rice. Golden in colour, mildly acetic and relatively sweet, it is used, sweetened, for sushi rice, and to season salads.

Chinese rice vinegar

Made from fermented rice. Generally milder and sweeter than malt and wine vinegars, there are three main varieties: black, with a complex, rich flavour; red, mild and slightly sweet; and white (depicted), mild and sweet.

Lemon juice

The juice squeezed from the lemon fruit. Highly acidic, it is used as a souring agent, a source of pectin for jams and jellies, to flavour and enhance, and to slow enzyme browning. Subsituted for vinegar in sauces, it results in a more delicate flavour.

Lime juice

The juice squeezed from the lime fruit. Very acidic (one and a half times more acidic than lemon) it is used, in the tropics, as a souring agent, to flavour and enhance dishes, and in drinks.

OTHER ACIDIFIERS

Verjuice/verjus

Literally 'green juice', an acidic liquid made from unripe fruit such as crab apples and, nowadays primarily, grapes. With a gentle lemony tartness, it is used in place of lemon juice or vinegar.

Rice wine

An alcoholic Japanese liquor brewed from fermented rice, there called saké. As a culinary ingredient it is used to marinate, tenderize and flavour food . Mirin is a Japanese sweet spirit-based cooking 'rice wine' used for marinades and glazes.

Worcester(shire) sauce

A proprietary bottled sauce, made from spiced vinegar by a maturation process, the exact recipe being secret. Of a thin consistency, highly concentrated and piquant, it is used world-wide as a condiment and seasoning ingredient.

Tomato sauce/ketchup

A thick sauce of tomatoes, cooked with sugar, vinegar, salt and spices, strained of solids. It is used both as a condiment and as an ingredient.

Light soy sauce

A sauce made from fermented soya beans, wheat and salt. The 'light' version is thinner, saltier and paler. It is used as a salty, sharp condiment and ingredient in Chinese and Japanese cooking when no change of colour is sought.

Dark soy sauce

A sauce made from fermented soya beans, wheat and salt. Brewed longer, with sugar or molasses added, the 'dark' version is thicker, sweeter and darker in colour so is used, as a salty, tangy condiment or ingredient, when a richer colour is sought.

Mint sauce

A thin sauce consisting of chopped spearmint leaves steeped in boiling water, sharpened with vinegar and sweetened with sugar. It is the traditional Anglo accompaniment for roast lamb.

Apple sauce

A purée of cooked apples, ranging in texture from smooth to chunky, either sweetened or unsweetened, and sometimes spiced. A traditional accompaniment to roast pork, it is also used for desserts.

Cranberry sauce

A jellied condiment, made by stewing pectin-rich cranberries in water and adding sugar; the crushed or whole berries are sometimes set in it. Sweet yet tart, it is a traditional American accompaniment to roast turkey.

Red pepper sauce

A sauce made with red sweet peppers or capsicums, often first roasted or char-grilled, as the primary ingredient. Puréed smooth, it is used to dress pasta, and accompany fish, meat and vegetables.

Jalapeño pepper sauce

A sauce with jalapeño chillies as the primary ingredient. With a smooth consistency and a hot, sweetish flavour, it is used as a condiment and a piquant, enhancing ingredient.

Tartare/tartar sauce

A mayonnaise to which chopped capers, gherkins, onion or shallot, herbs and sometimes, hard-boiled egg yolks, are added. It is served cold, traditionally with fried fish.

Barbecue sauce

A sauce traditionally made from tomatoes, onion, garlic, brown sugar, vinegar and mustard and, sometimes, other piquant seasonings. It is used both to baste meats to be cooked on a barbecue and to accompany barbecued meats.

Chilli sauce

A sauce varying from sweet and mildly pungent to fiery and astringent, with chilli as the common ingredient; some contain just chillies, vinegar and salt, others also include ginger, garlic, sugar and spices.

Teriyaki sauce

A Japanese glaze of dark soy sauce, sake, mirin and sugar applied to fish, meat or poultry in the final stages of grilling or pan-frying. It adds sweetness and gloss.

Black bean sauce

A paste of fermented, salted soya beans, rinsed, mashed and combined with garlic and oil, ranging from smooth to textured. With soy sauce, stock, rice wine, ginger and sugar, it flavours various Chinese steamed and stir-fried dishes.

Sweet bean paste

A sweetened paste made from dried beans: red, from adzuki beans, is a popular ingredient in Asian desserts; black, from fermented soya beans, is variously seasoned and used in Chinese cookery in marinades and as a condiment.

Satay/saté sauce

A thick chilli-spiced sauce based on coarsely ground peanuts (groundnuts), served as an accompaniment to small pieces of meat, marinated, threaded on a skewer and grilled, and as a dressing for the Indonesian salad, gado gado.

Plum sauce

A thick Chinese condiment, the key ingredients of which are salted plums, apricots, rice vinegar, chilli, sugar and spices. Sweet and tart, it often accompanies barbecued duck and roasted pork.

Sweet and sour sauce

A Chinese sauce combining a balance of sweet and sour ingredients. Commercial preparations typically include sugar, vinegar, red food colouring and a thickener. Used for dipping and cooking, it enhances rich meats, fish and vegetables.

Oyster sauce

A Chinese sauce made from extracts of oysters and brine,
coloured brown with caramel, and thickened with cornflour.
Used as a finishing seasoning, it imparts an enhancing salty,
savoury-sweet, meaty taste to meat and vegetables.

Hoisin sauce

A Chinese sauce of fermented soya beans, garlic, salt, sugar,
and typically wheat flour, vinegar and spices. Rich, sweetish
and tangy, it is used as a seasoning and as a dip for grilled
meats, and traditionally accompanies Peking duck.

Kecap manis

An Indonesian thick dark soy sauce sweetened with palm
sugar. Syrupy, sweet, rich, malty and slightly salty, it teams
well with meat, poultry and seafood dishes, colouring,
sweetening and caramelizing them.

ASIAN DIPPING SAUCES

Ponzu A Japanese sauce of soy sauce, lemon juice and/or rice wine vinegar, sake or mirin, dried bonito flakes and kombu (konbu).

Nam prik A Thai relish with a balanced taste of hot, salty, slightly sour and slightly sweet. At its most basic it contains shrimp paste, garlic, chillies, salt, lime juice, palm sugar, and, perhaps, fish sauce (*nam pla*).

Nuoc cham A Vietnamese sauce combining fish sauce, red chillies, garlic, sugar, lime juice, vinegar and water.

Goma-dare A Japanese sauce of ground toasted sesame seeds, soy sauce, mirin, sugar and dashi.

Powdered mustard

An English bright-yellow powder consisting nowadays of
white mustard seeds, dried, milled and sieved of their
husks, mixed with turmeric and wheat flour.
It is made up by mixing with cold water and leaving for
10 minutes. Pungent, with a sharp, clean, hot taste, it
is a classic English accompaniment to roast beef, ham
or sausages, and is used as a cooking spice.

Senf

German mustard paste, typically made with brown
mustard seeds, including the seed coat, wine vinegar,
sugar and often flavoured with herbs. Relatively dark,
smooth, with a mild, sweetish taste which masks the
flavour of the food it accompanies, it is a standard
condiment with German sausages.

Dijon mustard

A pale-yellow French mustard paste with AOC status,
made in a prescribed manner, generally near the
Burgundian city of Dijon. Brown or black mustard
seeds, soaked in verjuice, wine or vinegar, then crushed
and their seed coat removed, are mixed with salt,
spices, water and, possibly, sulphur dioxide. Pungent,
with an enhancing, clean, moderately sharp, hot taste,
it is used as a condiment and in sauces.

Bordeaux mustard

A brown French mustard paste, devised in Bordeaux.
Brown mustard seeds, soaked in wine vinegar, are
ground with their seed coats, and mixed with sugar and
herbs, often tarragon. Smooth and mild with a slightly
sour, masking taste, it is a suitable condiment for
charcuterie and sausages.

English mustard

An English mustard paste, also referred to as 'made mustard.' Yellow in colour and smooth in texture, it is pungent with a characteristically very sharp, hot, clean taste. It is eaten, sparingly, as the classic English accompaniment to roast beef, sausages and ham.

American mustard

An American mustard paste, made with white mustard seeds and coloured bright yellow with turmeric. Smooth in texture and generally very mild in flavour, it is particularly eaten on hot dogs.

Wholegrain mustard

A mustard paste in which the mustard seeds have been partially or coarsely crushed. Typically it has a speckled appearance, a thick, crunchy texture and a mild, nutty flavour. There are many variants; the French *moutarde de Meaux*, also known as *moutarde à l'ancienne*, is a long-established example.

Garlic and red pepper mustard

A mustard paste flavoured and coloured with garlic and red peppers. Mustard pastes of varying textures and pungencies have a range of flavourings added, including herbs such as tarragon, sweeteners such as honey, and further hot elements such as chilli, peppercorns and horseradish.

Horseradish paste

Grated horseradish root preserved in vinegar, and sometimes oil. It is used as a pungent condiment or mixed into cream or an egg liaison to accompany beef or fish. If cooked it loses its pungency.

Mayonnaise

An emulsion of egg yolks and oil, with lemon juice or vinegar, seasoned with salt, pepper and mustard. Consumed cold, it is used as a spread, a dressing, a sauce on its own and as a base for many other sauces.

Wasabi paste

A paste derived from the grated roots of the Japanese herb, wasabi, also called Japanese horseradish. With a pungent horseradish-like flavour it is used, sparingly, as a condiment, with sushi and sashimi.

Sambal oelek (ulek)

A basic SE Asian relish made from pounded chillies, traditionally unseeded, salt, and vinegar or tamarind. It is a potent condiment, and should be used, with caution.

Anchovy paste/anchïoade

A paste primarily of pounded anchovy fillets, typically mixed with vinegar, spices and water. With a pungent salty, fishy flavour, it is used as a spread and as a flavour-enhancing ingredient.

Tapenade

A Provençal paste of pitted black olives, capers, anchovies and, sometimes, tuna, seasoned with olive oil, lemon juice, brandy and aromatics. Intense and piquant, it is eaten as a spread, and a dip for crudités.

Sun-dried tomato paste

A commercial paste primarily of sun-dried (or artificially dried) tomatoes, plus oil and sometimes sugar, salt, vinegar and herbs. With an intense tomato flavour, it is used to enrich sauces.

Pesto

A thick uncooked sauce, associated with Genoa, traditionally of pounded fresh basil leaves, garlic, pine nuts, grated parmesan or pecorino cheese, and salt. It dresses pasta and gnocchi, and finishes minestrone.

Tikka paste

A commercial paste typically including ground coriander seeds, cumin, ginger, paprika, garlic, chilli, salt and oil, sharpened with lemon juice, tamarind or vinegar. Meat is marinated in the paste, then cooked.

Balti curry paste
A commercial paste with many variations, used to spice aromatically a mild curry freshly cooked in a wok-like karahi or balti.

Korma curry paste
A mildly spicy commercial paste intended for braised curry dishes, often including ground nuts and ground coriander, cumin, turmeric, ginger, cinnamon and cardamom.

Tandoori paste
A commercial paste used to marinate or coat meat to be cooked in a tandoor (clay oven). The gentle spicing typically includes ginger, paprika, garlic, cumin, turmeric, coriander seeds, cardamom, pepper and cinnamon.

Thai green curry paste
A green purée of fresh green chillies, galangal, lemon grass, coriander root, lime zest, shallot, garlic, shrimp paste, coriander and cumin seeds, salt and peppercorns. Hot and salty, it is fried with coconut cream as the basis of Thailand's most classic curry.

Thai red curry paste
A red purée of dried red chillies, garlic, shallots, lemon grass, galangal, shrimp paste and salt, with coriander root and seeds, cumin, lime zest, and peppercorns variously added. It is used for Thai red-curries, which are usually fried and coconut-based.

Harissa
A Tunisian fiery red paste of dried red chillies soaked and pounded with garlic, salt, coriander and caraway seeds, olive oil and, sometimes, cumin and mint. It flavours couscous and brochettes.

Shrimp paste
A thick odorous paste made from shrimp salted, fermented then dried. Pungent and salty, it is an essential ingredient in SE Asian cooking, used, raw or lightly roasted, to add depth of flavour. It is always eaten cooked.

Tahini/tahina
An oily cream/paste of ground, usually toasted, sesame seed kernels. It is used, raw and cooked, in Middle Eastern cookery, in savoury dips such as hummus, in sauces, and in confections like halva.

TWO MIDDLE EASTERN SEASONINGS

Tabil A fiery Tunisian paste of coriander, either fresh (cilantro), or seeds, caraway seeds, garlic, red pepper and chillies, ground or pounded.

Pomegranate molasses A thick, deep ruby syrup made by reducing the juice surrounding pomegranate seeds until concentrated. With a rich berry-ish fruity tartness, it is used in Middle Eastern cookery, notably in poultry dishes.

Mango pickle

A tangy, sweetish British condiment of mangoes, chopped and pickled in white vinegar spiced with mustard seeds, black peppercorns, salt, allspice berries and fresh ginger.

Pickled limes

A tart Middle Eastern pickle of limes, sliced, salted until limp and no longer bitter, layered in a jar, sometimes sprinkled with paprika, and covered with oil. It is served, as a contrast, with rice, meat or fish dishes.

Branston Pickle

A popular proprietary British condiment, the recipe of which is secret. A thick, sweet, tangy, spicy, sauce coats crunchy chunks of vegetable. It often accompanies cold meats, and cheeses.

Piccalilli

A mustard pickle of mixed vegetables. The UK version is chutney-like with a thick opaque vinegary sauce dominated by ground white mustard and turmeric. The US version is sweeter. In both, the vegetables, which often include cauliflower, are crisp.

Pickled peppers

Capsicums (sweet or bell peppers) and pimientos, of various colours, which have been deseeded, and often sliced, before being immersed in brine, then in vinegar. Sweet and sour, they are eaten as an accompaniment to cold meats.

Peppadew Piquante Peppers

A proprietary South African pickle of small round red 'piquanté' peppers in a mixture of vinegar, salt and sugar. Sweet, peppery, tangy and retaining some crispness, they are eaten whole, stuffed, chopped in salads and, often, teamed with feta cheese.

Sauerkraut

Shredded hard white cabbage, dry-salted and fermented, preserved by the resultant lactic acid. Still raw and crisp it needs simmering, after rinsing if too sour, before eating, famously accompanying charcuterie.

Gherkins

Small cucumbers (see p56) preserved in brine and/or vinegar, often with dill, ('dill pickles'), or other flavourings. They remain firm yet have tender skin. Classically they garnish cold meats and boiled dishes.

Pickled ginger

Ginger rhizomes salted, then marinated in sweetened vinegar. Made with rice wine vinegar, the Japanese version, thinly sliced, accompanies sushi and sashimi. The Thai version, made with coconut vinegar, accompanies curries.

Pickled onions

Small onions, peeled, dry-salted or brined, then preserved whole in spiced vinegar. Crisp with a pungent flavour, they are a popular accompaniment to cold meats and cheeses, as well as fried fish and chips.

Pickled walnuts

Whole immature walnuts, picked before their shells harden, brined, dried until completely black, then preserved in spiced, sometimes sweetened, vinegar. Tender, tart and spicy, they accompany cold meats and cheeses.

Capers

The small flower buds of the Mediterranean *Capparis* shrub, sun-dried, then pickled in salted vinegar, or dry-salted. Salty and slightly bitter, they flavour sauces and suit seafood. (Capers should be rinsed before use).

Pickled garlic

Whole cloves of peeled garlic, often blanched to reduce its pungency, then preserved in vinegar, sometimes sweetened and/or spiced. A crisp nutty accompaniment, it is also used in Thai food to temper flavours.

Pickled chilli

Fresh red or green chillies, preserved in brine and vinegar. Depending upon the type of chilli and vinegar, they may be very hot and spicy and should be used cautiously at first.

Sweet chilli sauce

A thick relish, at its simplest, of red chillies, palm sugar, white vinegar, fish sauce and salt. Sweet, sour and salty, it is used in Thai recipes for dipping, in dressings, and soups.

Chutney

A spiced, sometimes sweet, condiment with a jam-like consistency based on a non-specific combination of fresh and/ or dried fruits and vegetables cooked with, typically, malt vinegar, sugar, salt and piquant flavourings. Apples, raisins, apricots, onions or tomatoes are commonly used.

Mango chutney

A sweet, spiced, mango-based condiment, of Indian derivation. In commercial preparations, chunks of fresh unripe mango are cooked with vinegar, sugar, salt, garlic, ginger, chillies and spices to a pulpy jam-like consistency. It accompanies curries, and cold meats and cheeses.

Tomato chutney

A sweet, mild, thickish condiment based on tomatoes. Made to varying recipes, peeled tomatoes, green or, more usually, ripe, are cooked with sugar, vinegar, salt and spices, and sometimes other fruits and alliums. It teams well with cheeses and meats, both cold and hot.

Peach chutney

A pulpy, sweet, spiced condiment based on peaches. Fresh peaches, peeled, stoned and chopped, are cooked with vinegar, sugar, salt, and spices such as ginger, cloves and cayenne pepper to a jam-like consistency. It accompanies cold meats and cheeses.

Mrs HS Ball's Original Chutney

A popular proprietary South African spicy fruit condiment made with peaches and apricots, sugar, vinegar, salt and spices. It is served with curries, cold meats and cheeses.

Cherry chutney

A thick chunky, spiced condiment with pitted, generally sour black cherries, such as morello, as the principal fruit. Cooked with vinegar, sugar, salt, and spices, it has a sweet-sour flavour which complements ham, poultry, game and cheese.

Lime achaar

An astringent Indian condiment of limes pickled in their own juice. Fresh limes slit in four and stuffed with spices such as black pepper, chilli powder, garam masala, salt and, sometimes, sugar are left in the sun to mature. Sharp and hot, it is eaten as a flavour highlight as part of an Indian meal.

Mango achaar

An Indian oil pickle of mangoes, often highly spiced and very hot. Slices of unripe mangos are salted and sun-dried, then combined with such spices as turmeric, fenugreek, nigella, mustard and fennel seeds, plus chillies, and oil. It is eaten as a palate-stimulating condiment as part of an Indian meal.

Baby brinjal achaar

A hot Indian oil pickle based on baby eggplants/aubergines (brinjal). Degorged of excess juices, the eggplants are fried and cooked with spices, typically including a fried paste of mustard, ginger, coriander, cumin, fennel and chillies, sharpened with vinegar and tamarind. It is eaten as a palate-stimulating condiment as part of an Indian meal.

Black olives

The fully ripe fruits of the olive tree, cured in brine, sometimes
flavoured with aromatics. The fleshy pulp, enclosing an oval
stone, is soft, full of oil, and relatively mellow in flavour.
The many varieties differ in size, shape and nuance.

Stuffed olives

Cured green olives which have been stoned and the stone
replaced with pimiento, almond, capers, anchovy or tuna. Their
firm texture and sharp tang contrasts with the particular
stuffing. They are eaten as hors d'oeuvres and used as a
garnish, often sliced.

Green olives

The unripe fruits of the olive tree with their original bitter
glucosides removed by curing, with water, caustic soda or brine,
then pickled in brine, sometimes with aromatics. They are
firm-textured, with little oil, and a sharp tang.

Sun-dried olives

Ripe olives either dry-cured in salt then sun-dried, or simply
dried in the sun. Wrinkled, with an intense bitter taste, they are
sometimes then preserved in oil, with dried herbs and/or garlic.

Sweeteners & Flavourings

Sweeteners, self-evidently, give food and drink a sweet taste. Sweetness occurs naturally in many forms; pre eminent among them is sugar.

A simple carbohydrate, sugar itself takes several forms. Three sugars are of culinary importance: dextrose, commonly called glucose, is a monosaccharide (single sugar) present in plants and animal blood; fructose, also called laevulose or levulose, is a monosaccharide occurring in plants and honey; and sucrose is a disaccharide (double sugar) composed of glucose and fructose. Table sugar, 'ordinary' white sugar, is nearly pure sucrose. In a culinary context, the term 'sugar' denotes sucrose.

A diversity of plants is exploited for their sugars. One of the earliest sources of sugar was honey, processed by bees from the nectar of plants. The saps of trees, notably maple and palm, also yield sugars. Nowadays, sugar cane and sugar beet are the principal sources of sugar.

Sugars do not taste equally sweet. Fructose is one and three-quarter times as sweet as sucrose while glucose is three-quarters as sweet as sucrose, despite all having the same food value. Pure sugars merely taste sweet. Sugars with 'impurities', that is, anything other than sugar, also have nuances of flavour from the particular impurities.

As well as sweeten, sugar in high concentrations acts as a preservative. It is vital, in both roles, in jams, jellies and conserves.

This chapter also discusses ingredients used in conjunction with, and in the making of, sweet foods. Chocolate, not intrinsically sweet, is sweetened to varying extents. Essences extracted and distilled from plants flavour sweet foods without upsetting the balance of liquid or bulk of a recipe.

The consistency and texture of many sweet, and savoury, foods is achieved by raising agents and thickeners. Leaveners produce carbon dioxide gas which forms bubbles in a dough or batter, making it rise and become less dense. Gelling agents form a molecular mesh, transforming liquids into solid.

Pastries, doughs of flour and usually fat and/or water, encase, cover and constitute certain sweet foods.

White/granulated sugar

A fully refined white sugar, made from sugar cane or sugar beet, with medium-sized crystals. With virtually no taste other than sweet, it is the all-purpose, standard sugar.

Light brown sugar

A refined white sugar, coated with light cane molasses which imparts a delicate taste: golden granulated sugar (depicted) has medium-sized crystals; the fine-grained version is soft and moist.

Dark brown sugar

A refined white sugar, coated with a dark cane molasses, which imparts a rich caramel taste. Typically soft, moist and fine-grained, it is suitable for baking.

Demerara sugar

A partly refined, honey-coloured, raw cane sugar, originally made in Demerara (Guyana). It has a fine fudgy taste. With large, hard crystals it is dry, crunchy and suitable for table use.

Caster/castor sugar

A fully refined white sugar with very fine crystals. Fine enough to use in a sugar caster or sprinkler, it dissolves quickly so is excellent for baking. Called superfine sugar in the USA.

Muscovado/Barbados sugar

A partly refined, dark brown, raw cane sugar, originally made in Barbados. Moist, soft, and fine-textured with a distinctive rummy taste, it is used for baked goods such as fruit cakes and gingerbreads.

Sugar cubes/lump sugar

Granulated white sugar either moistened and pressed, or just compressed, into blocks. Used in hot drinks, especially in cafés, it can also be used to rub the oil from citrus zest.

Coloured sugar crystals

White sugar crystals which have been dyed a mix of colours. They are used for decorating cakes, biscuits and confectionery.

Palm sugar cakes/jaggery

The sap of various palm trees boiled down until concentrated, then set. Ranging from pale to dark brown, it has a distinctive, not cloying, nutty, caramel flavour. It is scraped from the often rock-hard cakes.

Vanilla sugar

White granulated or caster sugar which vanilla pods buried within have impregnated with the fragrance and flavour of vanilla. It imparts a perfumed vanilla sweetness to baking and desserts.

CANE SUGAR/BEET SUGAR

Most sugar is derived from sugar cane; sugar beet is the second most important source. Their extracted juices are progressively refined, by different initial processes, until white sugar is achieved. Chemically, the sugars from cane and beet are identical, and they taste the same. However cooks discern a difference in their performance; makers of preserves prefer cane sugar. The by-products of beet and cane white sugar are very different. The crude extract of sugar beet is so malodorous it is not consumed by humans. Thus the culinary semi-refined brown sugars and molasses syrups are all from sugar cane.

Light honey

A viscous sweet liquid made by honey bees from various flower nectars. It is extracted from the honeycomb and marketed in liquid (depicted) or creamed form. Because the colour, flavour and texture derive from the nectar, honey varies according to its source. Generally, lighter-coloured honey is milder in flavour than dark honey, though no less sweet.

Creamed honey

Pure honey which has undergone a controlled crystallization process. Fine starter crystals of honey stirred into liquid honey result in such small crystals that the honey seems smooth, silken and creamy, and has a pearly sheen. Seemingly solid but actually still liquid, creamed honey has a spreadable texture.

Dark honey

Honey with a dark colour and generally a more distinctive flavour than light honey, but equally sweet.
Due to its high fructose content, honey is sweeter than the equivalent quantity of sugar but, to the palate, honey seems less sweet because of the other flavouring substances it contains. In cooking, honey darkens food because it caramelizes readily. Honey is strongly hygroscopic (water absorbing), so baked goods containing honey keep well.

Honeycomb

Unprocessed liquid honey still in the hexagonal wax cells, the comb, as the bees created it. Sealed in, it has a better retention of flavour and aroma than extracted honey. The wax is edible though chewy. Chunk honey is liquid honey with a chunk of honeycomb in its container.

Rock candy/sugar candy

Large irregular sugar crystals made by the crystallization of a slowly evaporated saturated sugar solution. They are often grown on strings or twigs. Some are coloured, frequently brown, and may be scented. They are used to sweeten drinks, including certain liqueurs. Coffee sugar/crystals are smaller brown-coloured such crystals, used for sweetening coffee.

PRESERVING SUGAR

Preserving sugar is a fully refined coarse white sugar, used in the making of jams, jellies and marmalades. Because the large crystals do not clump together when stirred into a liquid they dissolve faster, reducing the need for stirring and the risk of caramelization and burning.

Icing/powdered/confectioner's sugar

A very fine, white sugar, made by grinding fully refined, usually granulated, sugar to a powder. To prevent it from lumping, it usually contains an anti-caking agent; it may still require sifting before use. Because it dissolves instantly, it is used in uncooked sweets where no granularity is desired, in icings/frostings and to dust sweet foods.

Fructose (tablets)

Fructose (powdered)

Fructose

A monosaccharide, naturally occurring in fruits and honey, also called fruit sugar and laevulose/levulose. Fructose in crystalline form has probably been isolated from sucrose, and divided into its component glucose and fructose. Fructose is much sweeter than sucrose (ordinary sugar), yet contains half the calories. Because it is hygroscopic (water absorbing), products baked with fructose stale more slowly.

Liquid fructose

A fructose syrup varying in sweetness and viscosity in inverse proportions. Because it inhibits other sugars from crystallizing, which gives a grainy texture, fructose syrup is used in making confectionery and ice cream. Made from maize starch, it is a form of corn syrup, but should not be confused with regular corn syrup, which is liquid glucose and is less sweet.

Almond essence

An intense flavouring based on the steam-distilled oil of bitter almonds. It is used, in small amounts, in sweet dishes, confectionery, and baking.

Vanilla essence

A distilled, concentrated vanilla extract. It is fragrant with a sweet, caramelish, faintly smoky flavour. True essences can usually be distinguished from artificial imitations by the label 'natural'.

Vanilla extract

An amber-coloured water and alcohol solution in which finely chopped, cured vanilla pods have been macerated to extract their flavour and fragrance. It contains at least 35% alcohol. The best contain little sugar; some contain thickening sweet syrups.

Orange essence

A flavouring based on the essential oil extracted or distilled from the rind/zest of oranges. Intensely orangey in aroma and flavour, it is used, sparingly, in baking and sweets.

Rosewater

The diluted distillate of fragrant rose petals. With a sweet, heady perfume, it is used extensively in Middle Eastern cookery to flavour pastries and sweets. Too much is cloying.

Grenadine

A concentrated syrup originally made only from pomegranate juice and sugar, but now also containing other red fruits. It is used to colour, sweeten and flavour desserts and, diluted, drinks.

Coconut cream

The thick opaque liquid which separates to the top of the liquid extracted when freshly grated coconut, kneaded with hot water, is squeezed though muslin. Tending to curdle, coconut cream is usually added at the end of cooking.

Coconut milk

The thin watery liquid which settles on the bottom of the liquid extracted when freshly grated coconut, kneaded with hot water, is squeezed through muslin. It is used for long simmering.

Dark (plain) chocolate

A solid mixture of cocoa liquor/solids (cocoa mass and cocoa butter ground from cacao beans) and sugar, often flavoured with vanilla and stabilized with lecithin. The higher the proportion of cocoa liquor/solids, the better quality, and more bitter, dark chocolate is. It is subdivided into bitter-sweet, semi-sweet and sweet.

Milk chocolate

A solid mixture of cocoa liquor/solids, milk solids and sugar, usually flavoured with vanilla and stabilized with lecithin. It is creamy and, with a lower proportion of cocoa solids/liquor, less intensely chocolaty than dark chocolate.

White chocolate

A solid mixture of cocoa butter, milk solids, and sugar, usually flavoured with vanilla and stabilized with lecithin; it contains no cocoa mass. It feels creamy in the mouth but lacks depth of flavour. It is more difficult to cook with than dark chocolate.

Chocolate drops
Small uniform-sized chunks of chocolate of various types and quality. Drops melt evenly and are convenient for baking, when intact chocolate pieces are needed.

Baking chocolate
Baking or 'cooking' chocolate has added vegetable fat instead of cocoa butter and a high sugar content. Although it lacks intensity and does not give a glossy finish, it does not need to be tempered to make it stable and is relatively easy to melt, and so is used for chocolate decorations. It is available in dark and milk versions.
'Couverture' has a very high cocoa butter content and no other fat, but may contain milk solids. Used professionally, it is intensely chocolaty and coats evenly and thinly, giving a glossy finish if tempered.

Drinking chocolate
A powdered mixture of cocoa and sugar and, possibly, depending upon the brand, lecithin as an emulsifier and milk powder. It is mixed with hot or cold milk to drink. With a typically low cocoa content it is not suitable for cooking.

Cocoa
An unsweetened powder ground from the residue of cacao paste after most of the cacao butter has been extracted. 'Dutched' cocoa is treated with an alkali which darkens its colour and aids dispersal in liquid. Cocoa imparts a strong bitter chocolate flavour.

Maple syrup

A syrup made by boiling down sap tapped from maple trees. A speciality of E. Canada and NE USA, it is graded according to colour and flavour, a light amber and mild flavour being considered best. Pure maple syrup is so designated; maple-flavoured syrup is less expensive corn syrup mixed with a little maple syrup.
With a sweet, characteristic flavour, it is eaten as a topping, commonly poured over pancakes, and used as a glaze and flavouring.
Maple sugar is sap boiled until almost all the water has evaporated.

Golden syrup

A British pale golden treacle, with a mild but distinctive, unmolasses-like flavour. It is an invert sugar syrup, a by-product of boiling down sugar-cane syrup to produce sugar; with the sucrose split into dextrose and fructose, it is much less ready to crystallize than sucrose. It is used as a sweetener in baking and as a topping for desserts.

Treacle

The British term for a viscous, sticky sugar syrup, a residue of cane sugar refining; it generally refers to the dark brown or black syrups known elsewhere as molasses. Its strong, sweet yet bitter taste is more pronounced the darker it is; because of its water content it is less sweet than sugar. It is used in baked goods such as gingerbread and treacle tart, and for making toffee.

Chocolate spread

A smooth, sweet chocolate-flavoured paste. Made in dark, milk, white chocolate or blended varieties, commercial versions commonly include cocoa powder and sugar blended with vegetable oil, milk powder, lecithin and vanilla, and sometimes also contain ground roasted hazelnuts. It is primarily eaten as a spread on bread but is also mixed with creams in desserts and may be diluted to a syrup.

Hazelnut spread

A smooth, sweet chocolate-flavoured paste mixed with ground roasted hazelnuts. Commercial versions also commonly include cocoa powder and sugar blended with vegetable oil, milk powder, lecithin and vanilla. It is primarily eaten as a spread on bread but is also mixed with creams in desserts and may be diluted to a syrup.

Peanut butter

A paste of ground roasted peanuts or groundnuts (see pp 60, 91). When crushed, the nuts release their oil which lubricates the mixture. Usually it contains some salt; some commercial varieties also contain vegetable oil, sugar, and emulsifiers. Its texture is either 'smooth' (depicted) or 'chunky', with nibs of crunchy peanut. It is primarily eaten as a spread, but is also an ingredient in cookies/biscuits and saté sauce.

Three-fruit marmalade
A British jam-like preserve made with three types of citrus fruit, such as orange, grapefruit and lime, combined and boiled with sugar. Characteristically including shreds, thin or thick, of peel, it is tangy with an underlying bitterness.

Orange marmalade
A British jam-like preserve made with oranges boiled with sugar, characterized by the shreds of orange peel included; bitter or Seville oranges make the archetypal bitter-sweet marmalade. It is primarily eaten spread on toast for breakfast.

Lemon curd/lemon cheese
A preserve made of eggs, sugar, butter, lemon rind and juice gently heated together until thick. Smooth, rich and tangy, it is eaten as a spread, on sponge cakes, and used as a tartlet filling.

Watermelon preserve
The rind (the white layer between the outer rind and inner flesh), and sometimes the deseeded flesh, of watermelon brined, then simmered and preserved in a heavy sugar syrup, usually sharpened with lemon and often ginger.

Raspberry jam
A sweet preserve of raspberries briefly cooked in their own juice with sugar; usually the seeds are left in. Of a semi-solid consistency, it is used as a spread, an ingredient in desserts, and in baking.

Apricot jam
A sweet pulpy preserve of stoned apricots, fresh or dried, cooked with water and sugar; the kernels are sometimes added for nuttiness. It is used as a spread, a baking ingredient and a glaze.

Strawberry jam
A sweet preserve of strawberries cooked with sugar and an acid such as lemon juice. Softly set, usually containing lumps of strawberry, it is used as a spread and an ingredient in desserts.

Fig jam
A sweet preserve of chopped figs, fresh or dried, cooked with water, lemon juice and sugar. Containing lumps of fig and speckled with tiny seeds, it is eaten as a spread.

Cape gooseberry jam
A sweet preserve of cape gooseberries (see p83) cooked with water, lemon juice and sugar. The broken cape gooseberries and their tiny seeds add texture to the semi-solid spread.

Blackberry jam
A sweet preserve of blackberries cooked with water and sugar; often apple is included. Softly set, and textured with pulp and pips, it is used as a spread and a dessert ingredient.

Baking powder

A raising agent consisting of an alkali (bicarbonate of soda) and acid (cream of tartar and/or sodium pyrophosphate), mixed with starch; when wetted and/or heated, they react together to produce bubble-forming carbon dioxide gas.

(Active) dry yeast

Tiny dehydrated granules of a single-celled fungus. Activated when mixed with warm liquid, the carbon dioxide they produce forms bubbles in, and thereby leavens, doughs. It is twice as potent as fresh/compressed yeast.

Cream of tartar

A crystalline powder of the acid salt, potassium bitartrate, made by purifying the precipitate of wine. Used with bicarbonate of soda as a raising agent, it also stabilizes beaten egg whites.

Bicarbonate of soda

An alkaline powder, also called baking soda or sodium bicarbonate. Mixed with an acid solution, it produces carbon dioxide so is used, with buttermilk, lemon juice or cream of tartar, as a baking leavener.

Powdered gelatin(e)

Granules of protein derived from the collagen in animal tissue. It is swollen in cold water then heated, (not boiled) to dissolve. Virtually tasteless, it is used to set aspics, jellies and mousses.

Sheet/leaf gelatin(e)

Thin, brittle, translucent sheets of gelatin(e). It is softened in cold water, squeezed then blended directly into the warm liquid of the recipe to dissolve. It gives a superior result to powdered gelatin(e).

Agar-agar
A purified dried gum extracted from various seaweeds, available as powder, shreds or sticks. It has setting properties stronger than gelatin(e), withstanding boiling water and setting without refrigeration. Also called seaweed jelly, vegetable or Japanese gelatin(e).

Custard powder
Proprietary blends of cornflour and sugar, coloured and flavoured; it contains no eggs. Mixed with milk and heated, it thickens to a dessert sauce approximating real custard. It is also a baking ingredient.

Powdered egg
Hens' eggs, either whole or separated into whites and yolks, spray-dried and pasteurized. Reconstituted, they can be used similarly to fresh egg but do not aerate as well and their flavour is altered.

TIMING & TEMPERATURE MATTER
Yeast is inactive when frozen, but grows slowly when cool, steadily when warm (at 24°C/80°F), vigorously when hot (38°C/100°F) and is killed at 60°C/140°F.

Gelatin(e) melts at about 27°C/80°F, and sets at about 20°C/68°F; if boiled its setting ability is impaired.

Agar-agar dissolves at ±90°C/194°F, and sets at about 45°C/112°F; reboiling does not impair its setting ability.

Custard powder requires heat to thicken.

Bicarbonate of soda and **baking powder** containing cream of tartar react immediately they are moistened; once they are activated a batter should be baked without delay so the leavening effect of the gas is not lost.

Shortcrust pastry

A dough consisting of fat, either lard and/or butter, rubbed into sifted salted flour, and mixed with cold water. It is the basic pastry used for pie crusts, and has a crumbly tender texture. Enriched with egg and/or sugar it becomes rich shortcrust and sweet shortcrust.

Rough puff (flaky) pastry

A quickly made dough consisting of sifted salted flour, butter and cold water; cubes of butter are rolled into it, producing a rich short, yet flaky textured pastry, used for pie crusts.

Puff pastry

A rich, light dough consisting of sifted salted flour, cold water and butter mostly incorporated by repeated rolling and folding. Cooked, it puffs up to hundreds of crisp, flaky layers. It is used for delicate recipes, both sweet and savoury.

Phyllo/filo pastry

A Middle Eastern dough of flour and water kneaded and stretched until paper-thin. Unwrapped, it quickly dries out, becoming unworkable. The sheets are used buttered and stacked together; cooked, they comprise many crisp, flaky layers. It is the pastry used to make sweet dishes like baklava and apple strudel.

PASTRY TIPS

The key to light tender pastry is to avoid the development of gluten in the flour by keeping the dough cool (so the fat doesn't liquefy), and minimally handling the dough.

Roll with short, quick, light strokes, rather than long, heavy, steady ones. Lightly flour the surface so as not to alter the proportion of flour in the pastry. 'Rest' pastry after handling: if it is allowed to 'relax' between rolling out and baking it will shrink less.

Cut flaky and puff pastries with a sharp knife so as not to compress the layers and reduce their expansion. To 'flake' the cut edges, 'knock up' a series of shallow horizontal cuts with the sharp blade of a knife.

Cook all pastry in a hot oven; it will set quickly before the fat can melt and the dough shrink and collapse. To facilitate the steam which forces the layers apart, bake puff and flaky pastries with a pan of water on the bottom of the oven.

Pâte sucrée/sèche

A French rich, sweet shortcrust pastry made by mixing a mash of egg yolks, butter and sugar into salted flour. Used for sweet tarts, it is crisp and tender when baked.

Pizza base

A flat disc of yeast-leavened bread dough, enriched with a little olive oil. Of Italian origin and particularly associated with Naples, authentically it is baked in a blisteringly hot wood-fired brick oven. Mostly it serves as a base for various savoury toppings, often featuring tomato and a stretched-curd cheese; the Niçoise *pissaladière* is a similar use. A pizza base can also be folded over a filling as *calzone*.

Red wine

White wine

Brandy

Sherry

Vermouth

Rice wine

Stout

Ale

Lager

Schnapps

Vodka

Marsala

Madeira

Sweet sherry

Dessert wine

Sparkling wine

Port

Rum

Gin

Amaretto

Cointreau

Frangelico

Calvados

Limoncello

Kahlúa

Drambuie

Pernod

Eau de vie

Cherry brandy

Framboise

Angostura Bitters

Mirin (sweet saké)

Bibliography

Davidson, Alan. *The Oxford Companion to Food*, Oxford University Press, 1999.

Davidson, Alan. *North Atlantic Seafood*, Harper & Row, 1989.

Davidson, Alan & Knox, Charlotte. *Fruit; A Connoisseur's Guide and Cookbook*, Mitchell Beazley, London, 1991.

Vaughan, J.G. & Geissler, C.A. *The New Oxford Book of Food Plants*, Oxford University Press, 1997.

McGee, Harold. *On Food and Cooking; The Science and Lore of the Kitchen*, Harper Collins, 1991.

Ayto, John. *A Gourmet's Guide; Food & Drink from A to Z*, Oxford University Press, 1994.

Solomon, Charmaine. *Asian Food*, New Holland, London, 2005. (Previously published as *The Encyclopedia of Asian Food*, Hamlyn, 1997.)

Yee, Jennifer. *Discovering Asian Ingredients for New Zealand Cooks*, Random House, 2001.

Del Conte, Anna. *Gastronomy of Italy*, Prentice Hall Press, 1987.

Brooker, Margaret. *At Its Best; Cooking With Seasonal Produce*, Tandem Press 2003.

Brooker, Margaret. *New Zealand Food Lovers' Guide*, Tandem Press 2001.

Stobart, Tom. *The Cook's Encyclopaedia; Ingredients and Process*, Grub Street, 1998.

Stobart, Tom. *Herbs, Spices and Flavourings*, Penguin Books, Harmondsworth, 1977.

Herbst, Sharon Tyler. *The New Food Lover's Companion*, Barron's Educational Series Inc, 1995.

Larousse Gastronomique, Mandarin Paperbacks, 1990.

Rogers, Jo. *The Encyclopedia of Food and Nutrition*, Merehurst Ltd, 1990.

Alexander, Stephanie. *The Cook's Companion*, Viking, Australia, 1996.

Harbutt, Juliet. *Cheese; A complete guide to over 300 cheeses of distinction*, Mitchell Beazley, UK, 1999.

Androuet, Pierre. *Guide du Fromage*, Aidan Ellis Publishing Ltd, UK, 1983.

Masui, Kazuko and Yamada, Tomoko, *French Cheeses*, Dorling Kindersley, Great Britain 1996.

Italian Cheeses; A guide to their discovery and appreciation, Slow Food Editore, 2000.

Ridgway, Judy. *Judy Ridgway's best olive oil buys round the world*, Gardiner Press, UK, 2000.

Dolomore, Anne. *The Essential Olive Oil Companion*, Macmillan, Australia, 1989.

Mallos, Tess. *The Bean Cookbook*, Lansdowne, Sydney, 1984.

Owen, Sri. *The Rice Book; The Definitive Book on the Magic of Rice Cookery*, Doubleday, London, 1993.

Larkcom, Joy. *Oriental Vegetables; The Complete Guide for Garden and Kitchen*, John Murray (Publishers) Ltd, London, 1991.

Durack, Terry. *Noodle*, Allen & Unwin, Australia, 1998.

Alford, Jeffery and Duguid, Naomi. *Flatbreads & Flavors*, William Morro and Co. Inc, New York, 1995.

Kennedy, Diana. *The Cuisines of Mexico*, rev ed, Harper & Row, New York, 1986.

Bharadwaj, Monisha. *The Indian Pantry*, Kyle Cathie Ltd, Great Britain, 1996.

Yan-kit So, *Classic Food of China*, Macmillan, London, 1992.

Thompson, David. *Thai Food*, Penguin, Australia, 2002.

Roden, Claudia. *The New Book of Middle Eastern Food*, Penguin, Harmondsworth,1986.

Roden, Claudia. *Book of Jewish Food*, Viking, UK, 1997.

Wolfert, Paula. *Couscous and other good food from Morocco*, Harper & Row, New York, 1973.

Field, Carol. *The Italian Baker*, Harper Collins, New York, 1985.

Brettschneider, Dean and Jacobs, Lauraine. *The New Zealand Baker*, Tandem Press, Auckland, 1999.

Collister, Linda and Blake, Anthony. *The Bread Book*, Conran Octopus, London, 1993.

Helou, Anissa. *Lebanese Cuisine*, Grub Street, London, 1994.

Bareham, Lindsey. *In Praise of the Potato*, Grafton Books, London, 1991.

Bareham, Lindsey. *The Big Red Book of Tomatoes*, Michael Joseph, London, 1999.

Bareham, Lindsey. *Onions Without Tears*, Michael Joseph, Great Britain, 1995.

Tannahill, Reay. *Food in History*, Paladin, UK, 1975.

Scott, Maria Luisa and Denton, Jack. *The Complete New Book of Pasta*, Morrow, USA, 1985.

Carluccio, Antonio. *A Passion for Pasta*, BBC Books, London 1993.

Carluccio, Antonio. *A Passion for Mushrooms*, Pavilion Books, Great Britain, 1990.

Carluccio, Antonio. *Antonio Carluccio's Vegetables*, Headline, London, 2000.

Grigson, Jane. *The Mushroom Feast*, Penguin Books, Great Britain, 1978.

Grigson, Jane. *Jane Grigson's Vegetables Book*, Penguin Books, London, 1980.

Grigson, Jane. *Jane Grigson's Fruit Book*, Penguin Books, London, 1983.

Grigson, Jane. *Jane Grigson's Fish Book*, Michael Joseph, London, 1993.

Della Croce, Julia. *Pasta Classica: The Art of Italian Pasta Cooking*, Chronicle Books, San Francisco, 1987.

Miller, Mark. *The Great Chile Book*, Ten Speed Press, California, 1991.

Gourley, Glenda. *Vegetables: a user's guide*, NZ Vegetable & Potato Growers' Federation Inc, 2003.

Grigson, Sophie. *Eat Your Greens*, Network Books, London, 1993.

Grigson, Sophie. *Sophie Grigson's Meat Course*, Network Books, London, 1995.

Bissell, Frances. *The Real Meat Cookbook*, Chatto & Windus, London, 1992.

Cordon Bleu, Meat Cookery, BPC Publishing Ltd, London, 1971.

Hippisley Coxe, Antony & Araminta, *Book of Sausages*, St Edmondsbury Press Ltd., Suffolk, 1994.

McAndrew, Ian. *Ian McAndrew on Poultry and Game*, Hamlyn, Great Britain, 1990.

Cox, Nicola. *Nicola Cox on Game Cookery*, Victor Gollancz Ltd, London, 1989.

Keville, Kathi. *The Illustrated Herb Encyclopedia*, Simon & Schuster, Australia, 1991.

Hemphill, John & Rosemary. *Complete Book of Herbs*, Chancellor Press, London, 1995.

Holt, Geraldine. *Geraldine Holt's Complete Book of Herbs*, Conran Octopus, London, 1991.

Boxer, Arabella. *The Hamlyn Herb Book*, Hamlyn, London, 1996.

Man, Rosamond and Weir, Robin. *The Compleat Mustard*, Constable, London, 1988.

Hemphill, Ian. *Spice Notes*, Macmillan, Australia, 2000.

Norman, Jill. *The Complete Book of Spices*, Dorling Kindersley, Great Britain, 1990.

Coady, Chantal. *Chocolate: The food of the Gods*, Pavilion Books, London, 1993.

McFadden, Christine and France, Christine. *The Ultimate Encyclopedia of Chocolate*, Lorenz Books, London, 1997.

Nice, Jill. *The Complete Book of Home-Made Preserves*, Harper Collins, Great Britain, 1995.

Downer, Leslie. *At the Japanese Table; New and Traditional Recipes*, Chronicle Books, San Francisco, 1993.

Salaman, Rena. *Greek Food*, Fontana, UK, 1983.

Casas, Penelope. *The Foods and Wines of Spain*, Penguin, London, 1985.

Owen, Sri. *Indonesian Food and Cookery*, Prospect Books, London, 1986.

Taneja, Meera. *Indian Regional Cookery*, Mills and Boon Ltd, London, 1980.

Waldegrave, Caroline and Jackson, CJ. *Leith's Fish Bible*, Bloomsbury, London, 1995.

Ingram, Christine. *The World Encyclopedia of Cooking Ingredients*, Hermes House, London, 2004.

Werle, Loukie. *Australasian Ingredients*, Gore & Osment Publications, Australia, 1997.

Newton, John (ed). *Food, the Essential A-Z Guide*, Murdoch Books, London, 2001.

Ferguson, Clare. *Food for Cooks*, Jacqui Small, London, 2003.

Pienaar, Heilie. *The Karan Beef Cookbook*, Struik, Cape Town, 2003.

Ward, Susie; Clifton, Claire and Stacey, Jenny. *The Gourmet Atlas*, Apple Press, London, 1997.

More ingredients

Annatto An orange-red food colour extracted from the seeds of a tropical American tree. Used to colour foods, including Cheshire cheese, it has largely been replaced by beta carotene.

antipasto An Italian term for a selection of appetizers served before a meal. Typical elements of an antipasto platter are cured meats, anchovies, olives, tomatoes, marinated vegetables and seafood.

Asian vegetables Various greens used in Asian cookery, including bok choy (Chinese chard, pak choy), Chinese broccoli (Chinese kale, gai lan), Chinese cabbage (celery cabbage, Chinese leaves), choy sum (Chinese flowering cabbage), gai choy (mustard greens, Oriental mustard), and tatsoi (rosette pak choy).

baked beans Haricot (navy) beans cooked in a tomato sauce, and usually canned. Traditional Boston baked beans are prepared in a sauce of molasses, sugar and spices.

bean curd A white cheese-like curd made from soya beans. Called *doufu* in China and *tofu* in Japan, it is bland in taste, but readily absorbs flavours. It is sold in vacuum-packed blocks or tubs of water. The texture can be either soft (silken), suitable for use as a dairy substitute, or firm, ideal for stir- or deep-frying. It is an excellent source of protein and is low in fat.

bread A staple food, at its most basic, from flour or meal, and water. Leavened breads are raised with yeast or baking soda to give them a lighter texture; flat breads are unleavened (not raised).

candlenut Tropical tree nuts, having a large hard, round fruit encasing one or two waxy, white kernels, resembling walnuts, that contain a toxin which renders them unsuitable for eating when raw. Once roasted, the nuts are cracked and the kernels sautéd, crushed with other ingredients, to produce an aromatic mixture used, fried, in Indonesian dishes.

carob The fruit of native Mediterranean tree, used a substitute for cocoa and chocolate in cakes, biscuits and puddings. It is available as powder, bars and drops. It contains less (almost no) fat than chocolate and no caffeine.

cassava A starchy, tuberous root with thick skin and creamy white flesh, grown and eaten as a staple vegetable in Africa and Central America. There are two basic varieties, sweet and bitter. Cassava requires proper preparation as it contains a glucoside that reacts with enzymes to produce poisonous prussic acid, which is driven off by heat and is soluble in water. If carried out correctly, the various forms of processing (peeling the root, washing, boiling, toasting and fermentation) remove toxicity. Dried cassava is processed to make a flour, and the leaves are harvested as vegetables. Also known as manioc, yuca.

chayote This pear-shaped fruit goes by many names, including custard marrow, christophine, choko and vegetable pear. Green, with firm white flesh and a subtle taste of marrow or cucumber, it can be prepared much like summer squash, or peeled and eaten raw in salads. It should be prepared under running water, as the skin secretes a sticky substance when cut.

chervil A leafy herb with a delicate flavour of parsley and anise. One of the classic *fines herbes*, it is used, with tarragon, for béarnaise sauce, and goes well with creamy dishes, but should be added just before serving to preserve its flavour.

chestnut A sweet nut of the genus Castanea, with a glossy brown outer skin and difficult-to-remove inner pellicle. Unlike other nuts, chestnuts contain mostly starch and little oil. As well as roasted in the shell to be eaten out of hand, they are used, cooked, both whole and puréed, in savoury and sweet preparations. They have an affinity with brassicas, mushrooms, poultry and game, chocolate, cream and red wine. Chestnut flour was an historical staple in parts of Italy and France.

chickpea flour Whole chickpeas ground into a fine flour (also called gram flour, besan flour and channa powder). It is used to make breads and bhaja (pieces of vegetable or fish dipped in batter and fried), as well as for thickening.

cider The juice from apples, naturally fermented to produce a fruity, alcoholic drink, both effervescent and still. It is used in the cooking of Normandy and Brittany, in northern France, and in southern England. Perry is a similar drink made with pears. In North America, cider refers to unfermented apple juice.

coffee Raw coffee beans are washed, fermented, husked, dried, roasted, then blended with other beans for flavour and variety, before being ground, mixed with water and heated to become the drink, coffee. For cooking, use very strong coffee, as this will give both colour and flavour.

dill pickles Small cucumbers pickled in brine flavoured with dill seeds, garlic, spices and salt. They are popular in Jewish and North American cuisine.

dolmades Stuffed vine leaves. Fresh leaves must be blanched to soften them, but those sold in brine need only be rinsed before use to remove the salt. Also known as dolmas, dolmathes.

durian A large fruit covered with close-set hard spines, cream-coloured flesh, and sticky pulp surrounding the seeds, which is eaten or cooked, often in rice dishes. Native to Southeast Asia, it is notorious for its odour, but loved for its rich custard-like texture and unique flavour, evoking comparisons with many fruits.

endive A salad leaf which, despite its delicate, frilly appearance, has a robust, slightly bitter, taste and crunchy texture. It is also called curly endive and frisée. Batavia endive, crunchier with broader leaves, is also known as escarole and Batavia.

feijoa A fruit, oval in shape, with tough, green skin and soft, granular white flesh surrounding a pulp containing many tiny, white seeds, with a unique aromatic flavour. Ripe when slightly soft and very aromatic and the jellied sections of the flesh are clear, they are eaten raw, and baked.

Florence fennel (*finnocchio*) The swollen stem base of the plant, used as a vegetable. With a crisp texture akin to celery and a sweet, anise-like flavour, it is assertive when eaten raw, becoming mellow when cooked, either braised, baked, grilled, fried or steamed. It should not be confused with the herbs, bitter and sweet fennel, whose leaves and seeds are used for flavouring.

galangal A spicy ginger-like rhizome used in Southeast Asian cooking. It needs to be chopped finely before use, but is available dried, ground or in brine. Also known as Thai or Siamese ginger (*khaa*). It subdivides into greater or lesser galangal.

gremolata A mixture of chopped lemon zest, parsley and garlic, used, particularly in Italy, to garnish dishes, notably osso buco.

guacamole A Mexican dip of ripe, mashed avocado, with finely chopped chillies, onion, coriander (cilantro) and, sometimes, tomatoes, traditionally served as a relish with tortillas.

haggis The pluck (heart, liver, lungs) of a sheep, minced, mixed with oatmeal, onion, suet and seasoning, stuffed into a sheep's stomach and boiled. Originally a means of utilizing offal before it spoiled, it is nowadays traditionally served, in Scotland and elsewhere, at Burn's Night suppers, accompanied by bashed neeps (mashed swedes) and champit tatties (mashed potatoes).

hummus Puréed chickpeas flavoured with tahini (sesame seed paste), lemon juice and garlic. A Middle-Eastern favourite, it is normally served with pitta bread. Also known as houmus.

jackfruit A large fruit, native to India and Malaysia, with green, knobbly skin that turns yellow-brown as it ripens. When ripe it has an unpleasant odour, although the sweet, juicy flesh tastes similar to pineapple or banana. The unripe seeds and flesh can be eaten as a vegetable or made into chutney.

jellyfish Used in Asian cuisine, edible species are highly prized for their crunchy, resiliant texture. It is sold dried, needing to soaked, blanched and shredded before use, or vacuum-packed for immediate use.

jerk A Caribbean seasoning of dried chillies, allspice, bay leaves, cloves, garlic and ginger, used to flavour chicken and meat.

Jerusalem artichoke A knobbly tuber of the sunflower family with a mild, sweet, earthy, nutty flavour, that can be sliced and added raw and crisp to salads, boiled or roasted like potatoes, or made into soups and purées. Drop into acidulated water when cut to stop them going brown. Because the carbohydrates they contain cannot be digested by humans, they pass intact into the gut where they generate quantities of gas. This can be lessened by boiling.

kale An 'open-hearted' member of the cabbage family, with a stronger flavour, smooth or curly leaves of dark-green or purple, and lacking a solid centre or 'heart'. A hardy vegetable, it is popular in northern European countries. Use as cabbage. Also known as boerenkool, collards, cole, curly kale.

kimch'i Eaten by Koreans with practically every meal, kimch'i is a fermented relish made by steeping Chinese cabbage in brine with cucumber, onion, garlic, ginger, chillies and, sometimes daikon (oriental radish). Some versions include salted fish. Its strong smell and flavour are an acquired taste.

kohlrabi Literally a 'turnip-cabbage', a brassica with a globular stem, either green, white or purple. The crisp, mild flesh tastes like a turnip, and is eaten grated or sliced raw, mashed, or cooked in chunks. Kohlrabi is popular in continental Europe, particularly Germany, and in Asia.

kumquat Resembling a small orange, unlike citrus fruit, the pith, rind and pips can be eaten, alongside the bittersweet flesh. Simmer in sugar syrup and add to fruit salad, preserve in brandy, or use in marmalades.

lamb's lettuce A winter salad leaf, with spoon-shaped leaves and a nutty flavour. It is also called corn salad and *mâche*.

loganberry A hybrid of the raspberry and blackberry, and resembling both in flavour, they can be used raw and cooked. Like most berries, they are summer-ripening.

longan A native Chinese fruit, similar to the lychee, with smooth, leathery skin that changes from orange to brown when ripe, and fragrant, translucent flesh. The easily peeled fruit can be eaten fresh, out of hand.

loquat Small fruit with apricot-coloured waxy skin, often spotted with brown. The juicy, tart flesh contains large brown seeds. Eat raw, add to fruit salads or use for jams and jellies. They are soft and bruise easily, so are not widely grown commercially.

lotus A plant of the water lily family, with white and pink flowers and an edible root which displays a lacy pattern of holes when sliced. Lotus root is used in Chinese and Japanese cooking, as much for its decorativeness as for its crisp texture and delicate flavour. The root must be peeled before eating, raw or cooked, and can be bought fresh, dried, frozen and in tins.

makrut lime A small citrus fruit with knobbly, green skin. The leaves and zest are used, finely shredded or grated, in Thai and Southeast Asian cuisine. The leaves are available fresh or dried. Also known as kaffir lime.

mangosteen Despite its name, this fruit bears no resemblance to a mango, but is deep purple and round, with a thick, inedible skin that encloses soft, white flesh divided into segments. The texture is reminiscent of plums, the flavour is sweet with a hint of sourness.

merguez A North African sausage made from beef, spiced with red pepper or harissa (see p233) to give a characteristic red colour. Serve grilled, accompanied by couscous.

meze (mezze) Small snacks served with drinks. Meze dishes include meatballs, cheese, olives, marinated vegetables and dips like hummus, taramasalata and baba ghanoush.

mirin A Japanese sweet spirit-based rice liquor used in cooking, glazes and salad dressings. When mixed with soy sauce, it forms the basis of yakitori and teriyaki marinades. Sweet sherry can be used instead, but is a poor substitute.

mixed spice A traditional English blend, featuring ground coriander, cinnamon, allspice, cloves, nutmeg and ginger. it is used in baking and to flavour steamed puddings, hence the alternative names, pudding spice or apple pie spice.

MSG Monosodium glutamate, a flavour enhancer widely used in the food-processing industry, which can cause adverse reactions in some people. It occurs naturally in certain seaweeds, known as *konbu* in Japan. In Europe, it has the additive number 621, but products containing natural MSG do not have to be labelled.

mulberry Purple-black berries, similar to blackberries in size and shape. Red and white varieties are also found. Soft and delicate, mulberries are usually collected from suburban trees.

okra A slim ridged pod containing small white seeds. When cooked, it gives off a sticky, gelatinous substance used to thicken Creole and Cajun dishes such as gumbo. Okra is used, both fresh and dried, in India, the Caribbean, North Africa and the Middle East. Also known as bhindi, gumbo, ladies' fingers.

ostrich A large flightless bird, originally from Africa but now farmed in many countries. Its dark red meat is lower in fat than beef and is particularly good for stir- or pan-frying.

pandan leaf Long, flat, green leaves used in Asian cooking to wrap around meat or fish, creating parcels that are grilled, or crushed and added to rice or curries for flavouring. In Malaysia and Indonesia they are boiled to extract the colour, which is used for sweetmeats. Also called pandanus and screw-pine leaf.

parsnip A root vegetable with an earthy, sweet flavour. Related to carrots, they can be cooked similarly, although being tougher, generally require longer cooking. Containing natural sugars, they are ideal baked or roasted, as well as boiled and puréed. The first frosts of autumn concentrate their sweetness.

pastrami Smoked beef, cut from the underside of brisket and dry-cured in a mixture of sugar, spices and garlic before being smoked. Legendary in New York as the delicatessen speciality 'pastrami on rye'.

pepino A tropical fruit native to Chile and Peru, resembling a small cucumber in looks, with golden skin, usually streaked with purple. With a mild melon flavour, it can be used in fruit salads or eaten like a melon. Also known as melon pear.

piri piri Denoting a very hot, small chilli and a sauce of chillies and peppers, simmered in oil, and used to baste or accompany meat, fish or prawns. Of Portuguese African origin, piri piri is sold as a sauce and powder. Also known as peri-peri.

prickly pear The fruit of various cacti found in the deserts of Central America, southern USA, Australia, India, South Africa and the Mediterranean. The spiky, fleshy leaves vary from green, yellow, orange to red and the soft flesh resembles a watermelon or cucumber, with small, edible seeds. They can be eaten fresh, with lemon or lime juice, or cooked, often as jam.

proscuitto In Italy, the term for cured ham, such as Parma ham. Cooked ham is *proscuitto cotto* and raw ham is *proscuitto crudo*.

pumpernickel A dense, dark-brown wholegrain rye bread from Germany. It is usually sold and eaten in thin slices.

quince A relative of the apple and pear, used almost exclusively for cooking. Fragrant and golden when ripe, quince flesh remains hard and tart, but once baked or stewed, they soften, develop flavour and turn golden pink. As quinces contain large amounts of pectin they make good jams and preserves, such as the thick quince cheese also known as Spanish *membrillo*, French *cotignac* and Italian *cotognata*.

Quorn A proprietary meat-free product made from mycoprotein, a member of the fungi family. With the taste and texture of meat, the range includes cold cuts, burgers, sausages and cubes.

ras el hanout A Moroccan blend of many spices, usually including cardamom, nutmeg, allspice, cloves, ginger, black pepper, cinnamon, coriander and cumin seeds, cayenne pepper, and sometimes, rose petals.

ratatouille A Provençal stew of aubergines, peppers, tomatoes, onions and courgettes simmered in olive oil, eaten hot or cold.

reindeer A wild deer found mainly in the Scandinavian countries and Russia. With a pronounced, gamey taste, the lean meat can be cooked like venison, and is increasingly available smoked.

roe Hard roe is the eggs or spawn of a female fish. Soft roe is the sperm (milt) of a male fish. Roe comes from many species; caviar, from the sturgeon, is highly prized, but salmon, trout, herring and cod also produce roe. It is eaten raw and salted (as caviar), sliced and fried, or made into products such as taramosalata. In Japan it is used to garnish sushi.

saké An alcoholic drink from Japan, made from fermented rice. It can be drunk, hot or cold, or used in sauces and marinades.

salsa Meaning 'sauce' in Italian and Spanish, salsa is best known in Mexican cooking as a chunky mix of chopped tomatoes and vegetables, often ready-made, served with meat or alongside nachos (corn chips). Mexican *salsa cruda* includes chopped green tomatoes, chilli, onion and coriander. Italian *salsa verde* has parsley, capers, anchovies, garlic, olive oil and vinegar

salsify A root vegetable resembling a long carrot, with brown skin and creamy waxy-textured flesh. It can be boiled or baked, and used in soups and stews. When peeled, keep in acidulated water to stop it turning brown.

saltpetre Potassium nitrate, traditionally used to preserve food and give colour to cured meats such as bacon, but nowadays largely replaced by nitrate.

sambal A term for the condiments or side dishes accompanying Malaysian, Indonesian and Singaporean meals. There are many variations, both cooked and uncooked, freshly made and sold in jars. Sambal oelek, made with red chillies, vinegar and sugar, is a well-known version

samphire Two different plants: the Mediterranean variety (sea or rock samphire), is small shrub with long, thin, fleshy leaves, and an unpleasant odour that fades once it is pickled. It is eaten as an accompaniment to cold meats. Marsh samphire (glasswort), has bright-green, succulent stems, a salty flavour and crisp juicy texture. It can be steamed or boiled until tender and served with butter or hollandaise sauce, often with fish.

sapodilla A round or oval-shaped tropical fruit with rough, brown skin enclosing soft juicy yellowish- or pinkish-brown pulp with a sweet aroma and slightly granular texture. It is astringent and bitter when unripe. Also known as chiku, naseberry, zapote.

sapote Various tropical fruits from Latin America, not all of which are related, but which share similar characteristics. The black sapote, from Mexico, has chocolate-brown flesh used in ice cream and cakes, often flavoured with vanilla or rum. It is also known as black persimmon or chocolate pudding fruit. The mamey sapote (chicomamey), from the West Indies, has thick rough brown skin and aromatic salmon-pink flesh with four large seeds. It can be eaten out of hand or used for ice creams or preserves. White sapote are plum-shaped and turn yellowish when ripe, the flesh having a creamy texture and a pear-like flavour.

satay Threaded skewers of beef, chicken or seafood, marinated and grilled. A speciality of Malaysia, Thailand and Indonesia, satays are often accompanied by peanut sauce for dipping.

sea cucumber Not a vegetable, but a worm-like sea creature, prized in Asia for its texture and flavour. It is usually bought dried, and soaked in water before further cooking. With a high protein content, it is considered nutritious. In Japan, it is eaten raw, thinly sliced, with vinegar and soy sauce.

shellfish Any aquatic animal covered by a shell, particularly those used for cooking; a category that includes crustaceans (crabs, lobsters, prawns and shrimps), abalone, scallops, mussels, sea urchins, oysters, periwinkles and clams.

shoyu A pure form of Japanese soy sauce, containing defatted, steamed soya beans and a higher percentage of roasted cracked (crushed) wheat than most soy sauces. It is less salty than dark soy sauces, with a more delicate taste. (See also tamari.)

snail Although most commonly associated with France, snails are also cultivated in other countries. Most often bought canned, and classically served with garlic butter, the flesh has a firm texture and sweet flavour. Also known as escargot.

soffritto (sofrito) An Italian and Spanish term for an aromatic mixture of finely chopped garlic, onion, carrot, celery, tomatoes or peppers, slowly cooked in oil, and used as a base for stews, soups and sauces. In Central American and Caribbean cooking, pork and ham are often added.

spring greens Young cabbages and other brassicas, harvested while the leaves are loose, before a heart forms. They are lightly boiled and tossed in butter. Varieties include collards, sugar loaf cabbage and curly kale.

sprouts (bean sprouts) The germinated seeds of peas, beans and grains, eaten raw in salads, in stir-fries and Asian dishes. Some of the best-known spouts include alfalfa, cress, mung beans, lentils, sunflower, mustard, chickpeas, and soya beans.

sushi A Japanese speciality, consisting of vinegared rice, shaped into mounds or rolls and encasing, or enclosed by, ingredients such as thin slices of fresh fish or seafood, vegetables, bean curd and omelette. The finished shape may be wrapped in sheets of toasted seaweed (nori), and served with pickled ginger and wasabi (a hot paste). There is an art to making sushi and the best Japanese chefs undergo extensive training.

Tabasco The trade name of a bottled hot pepper sauce made on Avery Island, Louisiana, by the McIlhenny family. The ingredients include chillies, salt and vinegar. Green Tabasco is milder.

tamari A pure Japanese soy sauce made with only soya beans, whole or defatted, and excluding wheat. It is dark in colour. True tamari is rare, even in Japan. (See also shoyu.)

taro Collectively, a group of tropical tubers, and a staple food of Asia-Pacific, West Africa and the West Indies. The many varieties should all be cooked before eating, usually by boiling or steaming, to eliminate calcium oxalate that accumulates under the skin and gives an acrid taste. Once cooked, taro has a similar taste and texture to potato. Powdered taro root can be used in the same way as arrowroot. In the West Indies, the young leaves, called callaloo, are prepared as a vegetable, but also require careful cooking to remove the calcium oxalate.

teff (tef) A cereal grain from North Africa, particularly Ethiopia. A staple food, it is ground and made into a flat bread (injera).

tomatillo A physallis fruit, this relative of the tomato is used as a vegetable, either raw or cooked. The thin-skinned fruit varies in colour from green and yellow to purple; the flesh is pale green or yellow with many tiny seeds. A key ingredient in Mexican salsa verde, it is also used for guacamole and chutneys. Other names are Mexican husk tomato and green tomato.

TVP An acronym for textured vegetable protein, extracted from soya beans. The resulting paste is coloured, sometimes flavoured, and given texture to resemble ground (minced) meat. It is sold in dried form to be reconstituted through cooking, or pre-formed into cubes and 'steaks'. It is also used as an extendder in processed meats, such as sausages.

ugli fruit Native to Jamaica, this citrus fruit is a member of the tangelo family. A large fruit, resembling a grapefruit but with thick, bunched up skin, it has a mandarin-like taste. Easily peeled, the segments can be eaten out of hand.

umeboshi A variety of apricot, but often called a Japanese plum, this small, tart fruit is pickled in brine or salted and dried. The colour comes from the inclusion of red shiso leaves. They are mostly eaten as a pickle with rice, or served in green tea, often at breakfast. Umesu is an alkaline vinegar made with the brine in which the ume are soaked.

vine leaves Fresh vine leaves are sometimes cooked as a vegetable, but the best-known usage is in dolmades, when the leaves are stuffed with a mixture of meat or rice. Fresh leaves must be blanched, and tinned leaves rinsed, before use.

water chestnut Best-known as an aquatic plant, native to Southeast Asia, the European version, called water caltrope, and the singhara nut of Kashmir both come from the same family. (None should be confused with the Chinese water chestnut.) The walnut-sized corms have a dark brown skin, white flesh and a floury texture. They are bought fresh or canned, and roasted or boiled before use in stir-fries, wontons and sweet dishes.

Index

Photographic credits

All photography by NHIL/Neil Hermann, with the exception of the photographers listed below.
Copyright rests with these agents and/or photographers.

Page 9 - Digital Source
Pages 10 & 188 - Gallo Images/Gettyimages.com

Acknowledgements

The publishers would like to thank the stylists, Amelia Zelezniak in Cape Town, and Christine Cavaleros in London, for sourcing and styling the ingredients depicted in this book.